RAG DARLINGS

~ RAG DARLINGS ~
DOLLS FROM THE FEEDSACK ERA

BY GLORIA NIXON

Editor: Deb Rowden
Designer: Kelly Ludwig
Photography: Aaron T. Leimkuehler
Copy Editor: Gail Borelli
Photo Editor: Jo Ann Groves

Published by:
Kansas City Star Books
1729 Grand Blvd.
Kansas City, Missouri, USA 64108

First edition, first printing

ISBN: 978-1-61169-147-4

Kansas City Star Quilts moves quickly to publicize corrections to our books. You can find corrections at KansasCityStarQuilts.com, then click on "Corrections."

Library of Congress Control Number: 2014952552

Printed in the United States of America by Walsworth Publishing Co., Marceline, MO

To order copies, call StarInfo at 816-234-4473.

KANSAS CITY STAR
QUILTS
Continuing the Tradition
KansasCityStarQuilts.com

~ TABLE OF CONTENTS ~

~ ACKNOWLEDGMENTS ~

Many shared in making this book a reality. It is with deep gratitude that their assistance and hard work are acknowledged.

Kenneth and Robert Rees, great-grandsons of Isaac W. and Catherine Rodkey, granted permission to use the Rag Darling name on the book cover and expressed their happiness for the dolls to be shared with readers. Kenneth Rees suggested reference material that helped clarify dates and made a difference in the story.

When it seemed impossible to locate some of the dolls, many offered help. I would like to express a special thank you to the following for sharing photographs, research, background material and valuable time:

- Arabella Grayson, writer and curator of "Two Hundred Years of Black Paper Dolls"
- Amy Neely, business manager of Patee House Museum and Jesse James Home in St. Joseph, Missouri
- Memorial Hall Museum, Deerfield, Massachusetts
- Pilgrim Hall Museum, Plymouth, Massachusetts
- Wesley J. Fehsenfeld, The Uhlmann Company
- Korrie Wenzel, publisher, The Daily Republic
- ConAgra Foods Inc.

Fellow feedsack and quilt historians Edie McGinnis, Donna di Natale and Christine Motl volunteered doll sacks and so much more. Whether I needed thoughts on research, answers to questions or a dozen other things, they responded cheerfully. Christine mailed a doll so I could see it in person, identified the Wendy Werthan wardrobe sacks and sent photographs of one from her own collection. Donna emailed when she found the rare Certified Pig doll and asked if I wanted to borrow it. By the end of the day, book-ready photographs were in my inbox. When the manuscript was nothing more than a casual comment over lunch, Edie said, "Whatever I have is yours," and meant it. She graciously made time for conversations about doll finds and lent sacks for the photo shoot.

I owe my family profound thanks, especially my husband, Roger. He rearranged his schedule so I could have quiet time to work and never complained when yet another doll came through the door. "Tell me about this one," he'd say. Our daughter, Amy, was enthusiastic and supportive. She stayed on the lookout for dolls and found Miss Phoebe Primm in an antique store in Kansas City.

The staff at The Kansas City Star did an outstanding job. Each one deserves more thanks than I can ever give: Aaron Leimkuehler for photography; Jo Ann Groves for production assistance; Gail Borelli for her copyediting; and Kelly Ludwig for the lovely page design. I would also like to thank Edie McGinnis, who championed the book and let me know that she believed in it. Thank you!

It was a privilege to be teamed with editor Deb Rowden. I have a number of the quilt books she authored or edited in my library and was excited at the thought of working with her. Deb's experience put me at ease. With a grateful heart, I thank her for the professionalism, support and hard work she gave to the project.

A special thank you is reserved for publisher Doug Weaver, who looked beyond a few sentences in the proposal to a book filled with more dolls than I already had. I humbly thank him for the opportunity and the trust.

~ ABOUT THE AUTHOR ~

G loria Nixon is a feedsack historian and collector of patterned sacks, flour sack dolls, feed ephemera and old quilt patterns. She is a member of the American Quilt Study Group and the author of "Feedsack Secrets: Fashion From Hard Times." Gloria and her husband, Roger, live on the Kansas prairie and enjoy quiet moments together on the front porch, watching wild turkey, deer and red foxes at play.

~ DEDICATION ~

Dedicated to my daughter, Amy Lynn Nixon, and the memories we share of days spent playing with dolls.

Photo by Roger Nixon

~ INTRODUCTION ~

Dolls hold a cherished place in family history. Almost 400 years ago, a simple rag doll made of wool, linen and cotton was carried in the arms of a young girl as she left the Mayflower and began life in the New World. Over the next 200 years, children played with similar dolls fashioned from scarce pieces of cloth and bits of rag in the household scrap basket.

Yard goods were expensive, imported from Britain at a cost far beyond the means of many colonists. It was not until after the Revolutionary War and the War of 1812 that the number of American textile mills was sufficient to produce reasonably priced goods. During the second half of the 1820s, machines made the inexpensive cotton often referred to as calico. Finally, patterned cloth was within reach of many family budgets.

With fabric readily available, women's magazines and books began to offer articles on sewing. In 1831, "The American Girl's Book" gave detailed instructions for making homemade rag dolls. It suggested using watercolors to paint facial features and hair. Attention was directed to accessories such as gloves, boots and stockings, with a reminder to dress her in a "nice frock and petticoats." Calico and gingham quickly became favorites for doll clothes.

Several decades later, the domestic sewing machine came on the scene and made easy work of home sewing projects. By the last quarter of the 19th century, many families owned their own machines. It was during this time that the commercial cut-and-sew doll was born. With the help of her modern sewing machine, Mother could snip out the pieces and sew and stuff the doll in minutes instead of hours.

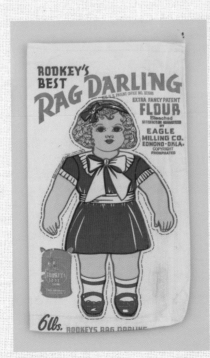

Advertisers were watching. When they saw the potential to introduce new products and expand their customer base, cut-and-sew dolls, sometimes entire families of them, were printed with a company or product name. Their ad, "Such delightful toys for so little money," appealed to parents everywhere.

Flour and cereal millers soon used these brightly colored dolls to promote their products. Aunt Jemima was first in a 50-year line of flour dolls. The Ceresota Boy followed. Early dolls were printed on flat muslin or linen sheets and sent to customers by mail, but it was not long before millers realized that a doll could be printed on the cloth sacks that held the flour.

Sugar millers joined the doll parade. During the depths of the Great Depression, an impressive series of 35 Sea Island Sugar dolls debuted at the California Pacific International Exposition. About the same time, an Oklahoma flour miller added beautifully detailed dolls to its sacks of flour, named them Rag Darling and launched an extensive advertising campaign.

Demand for the rag doll remained high throughout the rest of the Depression and World War II. More were yet to come. When millers of various foodstuffs ended the run, well over 100 dolls had been released. Most of those are shared here. It is my hope that you enjoy the story behind them and find it useful as you search for dolls to add to your own collection.

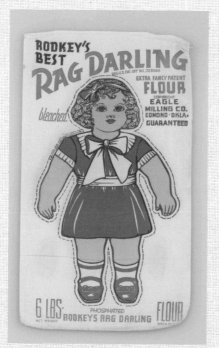

~ CHAPTER ONE ~
HOMEMADE RAG DOLLS IN AMERICA

*E*very little child loves a doll. Dolls have been made as long as there were materials at hand. Wood, ivory, leather, bone, scraps of cloth and fired clay were a few of the early materials used in doll making.

The oldest rag doll[1] still in existence was made in Egypt between the first and fifth centuries and can be seen at the British Museum in London. Coarse linen forms the head, arms, legs and body, which are stuffed with rags and papyrus. A single blue glass bead attached to the head, in the customary place for a hair ornament, suggests it was likely a female doll.

Early rag dolls are a rare find. Playtime, moisture and sunlight took a toll on the natural fibers in the cloth and filler. Over the centuries, most disintegrated. Those from more arid climates, such as Egypt with its dry, sandy soil, stood a better chance of being found intact centuries later and displayed in museums today.

Rag dolls were exposed to similar elements in the days of Colonial America. Most were played with well after they became tattered and soiled and eventually had to be discarded. The ones that survived allow us a glimpse into children's lives in early America.

Courtesy of Pilgrim Hall Museum, Plymouth, Massachusetts
Mary Chilton (1607-1679)
Netherlands, circa 1615-1620
Wool, linen, cotton
PHM #1584, Gift of Ruth and Walter Dower, 1982

EARLY RAG DOLLS IN AMERICA

It has been said the first rag doll in America was carried in the arms of 13-year-old Mary Chilton during the Mayflower voyage of 1620. Legend names her as the first woman to step ashore at Plymouth Rock. While that part of the story cannot be confirmed, we do know she endured brutal hardship the first winter in the New World, including the loss of both parents. When land was divided, she received her own allotment plus the two reserved for them. Mary lived a long and prosperous life with her husband and 10 children. Her doll is displayed at the Pilgrim Hall Museum in Plymouth, Massachusetts. An 1877 portrait titled "The Landing of the Pilgrims" is also on display there and shows young Mary stepping onto Plymouth Rock.

About 1770, a unique rag doll was made for Clarissa Field, a 5-year-old

[1] *Rag doll is a term used to describe a cloth doll stuffed with filler such as cotton, old rags, sawdust, bran, straw, etc. Many were marketed as cut-and-sew home projects, also called panel or pancake dolls. Some were printed with a company or brand name or were purchased through product advertising and can be called cut-and-sew advertising dolls.*

blind child from Northfield, Massachusetts. It is dressed in elaborate linen undergarments, including a corset with wood stays, bodice, drawers and two petticoats. The fingers appear different from the ordinary rag doll. Each is shaped individually and elongated, perhaps to stress the importance of touch to Clarissa. She named the doll Bangwell Putt and kept it until her death 80 years later.

Another doll known as Mollie Brinkerhoff, made of homespun linen stuffed with flax, dates to the Revolutionary War. As the story goes, the Brinkerhoff family of Long Island, New York, placed the doll inside a chest holding their most precious possessions and buried it before British soldiers landed there in the summer of 1776. The family fled, possibly to Connecticut, where other colonists sought shelter. Mollie survived and was reunited with her family after the war.

Homemade rag dolls were common during the 1800s. The nicely illustrated "The American Girl's Book: Or, Occupation for Play Hours," published in 1831, contains instructions for making several rag dolls. The jointed linen doll was appropriately named with 14 sections sewn separately, stuffed tightly with bran and then stitched together to form movable joints. When the doll was completed, "... her face must be handsomely painted in water-colours; so as to represent cheeks, eyes, nose and mouth; hair must also be painted to look as if curling all over the back of her head, and round her forehead. When the face becomes soiled, it can be renewed by sewing on a new piece of linen, and painting it again."

The faceless Bangwell Putt, 15.25" tall. The brown dress with acorn-like figures was added at a later date. Photograph courtesy of the Pocumtuck Valley Memorial Association, Memorial Hall Museum, Deerfield, Massachusetts.

Accessories were important, too. "You may make gloves for her out of the arms of old kid gloves, and also boots or shoes of the same. Her stockings may be made of the tops of fine old stockings. If properly drest in a nice frock and petticoats (like a baby for instance) this doll will look extremely well, particularly if her face is prettily painted; and she will be found an excellent plaything even for a little girl of seven or eight years old, who may take pleasure in making clothes for her."

The common linen doll was easy enough for the youngest seamstress. "These dolls are easily made, and answer every purpose for very small children. They may be of any size, from a quarter of a yard long to a finger length. Some little girls make a dozen of these dolls together and play at school with them."

Rag dolls ranged from elegant to lowly. Even in areas of the country where

Jointed linen doll, "The American Girl's Book," 1831

materials were scarce, a way could be found to make a doll. The mother from the poem on this page, "A QueerDoll," started with something unusual and turned it into a doll worth remembering. Perhaps you can guess what it was before the story ends.

CUT-AND-SEW RAG DOLLS

Common linen doll, "The American Girl's Book," 1831

Commercially made cut-and-sew dolls and toys were introduced during the 1880s and 1890s and almost instantly became a booming business. These dolls were printed in several colors, typically on linen or muslin, and stamped with instructions for cutting and sewing. Arnold Print Works, Art Fabric Mills, Cocheco Manufacturing Co., Selchow & Righter and the Saalfield Publishing Co. were just a few of the names involved in marketing high-quality cloth dolls.

Arnold Print Works of North Adams, Massachusetts, offered an impressive line that included the Palmer Cox Brownies, Columbian Sailor Doll, Our Soldier Boys, Bow-Wow, Tabby Cat and Little Red Riding Hood. Its jointed cloth doll, designed and patented by Charity Smith of Ithaca, New York, used small darts at

A postcard shows unidentified girls playing with life-size rag dolls, 1904-1918.

the elbows, knees, ankles and hips to give curves and a life-like form. "She'll love this one with all her heart, because it's pretty and won't break. Printed with permanent sanitary colors." Arnold Print Works filled customer orders on request for a brief time and then turned over all sales to dry goods retailers. Two jointed cloth dolls sold for 25 cents.

A QUEER DOLL

A queer little doll
In a very long dress,
But what it is made of
You never can guess.
Mamma was the person
Who thought of the plan,
She can find out a way
If any one can.
'Twas just after dinner
She brought from the table
The frame—you can guess it
Whenever you're able.
A bit of white cotton
Tied on with a thread,
And then in a minute
The doll had a head.
A stitch here and there—
Mamma knew the place
Where each should be set—
And the doll had a face.
A piece of white muslin
That came to the feet
Was sewed round the neck,
And the dress was complete.
A queer little dollie
It was, you will own,
When I tell you 'twas made
Of the turkey's wishbone.
—Joy Allison
"Wide Awake," November 1884

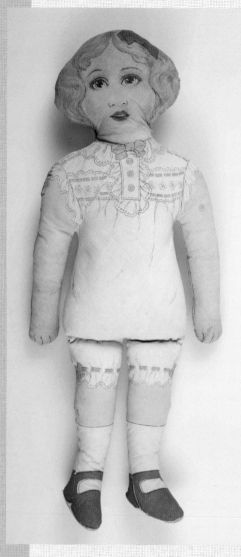

This blond 24" rag doll, possibly from Saalfield Publishing, is the same one in the photo with the two girls on page 11.

Arnold Print Works jointed cloth doll, 14" tall

Advertisement, Arnold Print

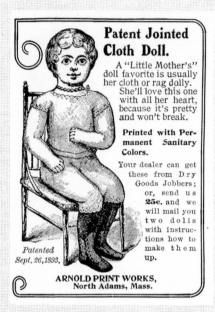

Patent Jointed Cloth Doll.

A "Little Mother's" doll favorite is usually her cloth or rag dolly. She'll love this one with all her heart, because it's pretty and won't break.

Printed with Permanent Sanitary Colors.

Your dealer can get these from Dry Goods Jobbers; or, send us **25c.** and we will mail you two dolls with instructions how to make them up.

Patented Sept. 26, 1893.

ARNOLD PRINT WORKS,
North Adams, Mass.

Works jointed cloth doll

Art Fabric Mills advertised a 30" tall, life-sized doll in 1900. "Baby's clothes will now fit dollie … If Mamma can donate one of baby's outgrown changes, that her little daughter can put on and off, button and unbutton to her heart's desire, the Life Size Doll will live in that child's memory long after childhood's days have passed away." It had golden hair, brown eyes, red stockings and black shoes. The price, which included two miniature dolls, was 50 cents by mail order. This full-page advertisement from 1905 (next page) offered the doll for a 2-cent stamp and made a request, "All we ask is that you show the doll to your friends and that you read our circular of sanitary cloth toys that we send with it … If you send 10 cents extra, we will send with the doll a pair of Good Luck Kittens printed on durable cloth." Directions for cutting and sewing the doll were printed on the cloth. The kittens have a patent of July 5 and Oct. 4, 1892.

A set from Art Fabric Mills called the Family of Dolls dates to September 1901. "They are the 20th century model of the old fashioned rag doll that Grandma used to make and would make Grandma open her eyes in wonder ... These dolls have rosy cheeks, beautiful hair, heads that will not break, eyes that will not fall in, nor suffer any of the mishaps that dollies are likely to encounter." This Mother doll has been referred to as Martha Washington, although advertisements call them Father, Mother, Brother and Sister. Each was made from extra-heavy sateen, printed in bright colors and dressed in continental costumes. This 1902 ad lists the price for the family at 60 cents and gives the address for mail orders.

Art Fabric Mills rag doll for 2-cent stamp, The Delineator, 1905

Mother doll from Art Fabric Mills, approximately 20" tall. The black sewing lines are visible. She was stuffed through an opening along the lower right side. Her feet are seamed at the ankle and shaped with cardboard. A black bow adorns each shoe.

Ad for Family of Dolls by Art Fabric Mills, 1902

A comic character, drawn by Carl Schultze for the funny pages, claimed a spot in the Art Fabric Mills doll line of 1903. Foxy Grandpa became an instant hit. A company flyer said: "This familiar caricature drawn by Mr. Shultz (sic) of the New York Journal appeals to the children. Grandpa is fat and funny. His bald head is a never ceasing source of amusement. He is dressed in a blue suit with the familiar spectacles, and the

Foxy Grandpa

Foxy Grandpa back

bunnie under his arm is the same drawn by Mr. Shultz in all his caricatures. Grandpa is 20" tall and almost as broad and guaranteed to stand much treatment from the young folks. Directions for making accompany each doll. Sent post paid for 25c."

Dean's Rag Book Co. was established in London in 1903. It built a fine reputation selling printed cloth books and a line of lithographed cloth dolls and toys called Knockabout Toys. "Dean's Rag Knockabout Toy sheets are real works of art, and make soft toys that cannot be broken, last a lifetime, and are produced in artistic colours on a strong cotton cloth by the same process as Dean's Patent Rag Toy Books." Its Dolly Dips the Seaside Doll dates to 1919 and was advertised as a rag character doll. A few from the same line were Gilbert the Filbert or the Nursery Knut, Florrie the Flapper, Curly Locks, Flaxen Flora, Darling Dora, Natty Nora and Laughing Laura.

Dolly Dips the Seaside Doll, about 19" tall uncut

Elms & Sellon of New York made the Standish No Break Life Size Doll marked, "Registered in England. Made in the U.S.A." The cloth is very heavy with sewing instructions in four languages. The doll measures 26" tall before sewing; two small ones are 8" tall. Newspaper advertisements for the Standish ran from 1912 to 1917 in the United States.

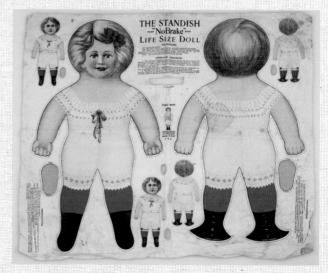

Standish No Break Life Size Doll

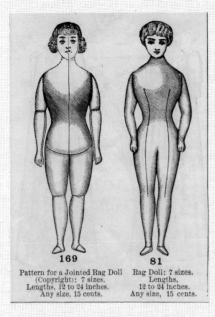

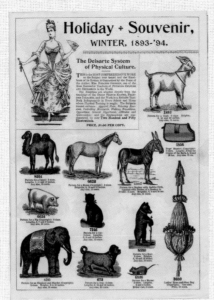

Child with stuffed cat, circa 1915

Butterick rag doll patterns, "Winter Holiday Souvenir 1893-'94" book

Butterick animal patterns, "Winter Holiday Souvenir 1893-'94" book, sizes ranged from 3" to 16" tall.

Butterick rag doll ad, The Delineator, 1907. "About 18" tall, printed flat in eight colors on durable cloth, quickly and easily made up."sizes ranged from 3" to 16" tall.

Young girl rocks a cut-and-sew rag doll, circa 1920

In 1882, Butterick Publishing Co. began selling patterns to make rag dolls and featured them in the December issue of its Delineator magazine. Seven sizes, from 12" to 24", were available for 15 cents per pattern. A year later, Butterick released the pattern for a jointed cloth doll. The company added an 18" doll, "printed flat in eight colors on durable cloth, quickly and easily made up," in 1907. "To teach the future mother to dress the future child, we have prepared the Butterick Rag Doll and a series of patterns of attractive Dolls' Dresses, etc. Remember it is but a step for the little ones from the making of pretty clothes for their dollies to the more useful accomplishment of making dainty garments for themselves and others." The rag doll and two sets of dress patterns sold for 25 cents.

THE CUT-AND-SEW ADVERTISING DOLL

Cut-and-sew dolls were popular and sold well, so it was only a matter of time before manufacturers found a clever new way to market them. The result was the advertising doll[2], which became an effective tool to sell everyday items used in the home. Grain, cereal, coffee, sugar, soap, dye, baby food and many more products promised a doll in exchange for a few cents, a package coupon or a box top. Sometimes the company name was printed on the front of the doll. Everywhere the child who held it went, so did the name. Children begged to have the same doll as a playmate down the street, and mothers bought the products to give them the joy of a little rag doll.

In 1903, the Korn-Krisp Co. of Battle Creek, Michigan, offered a large doll free with the purchase of two boxes of breakfast cereal. She is beautifully detailed in a lace and ribbon undergarment, red buttoned shoes and stockings. Several pieces make up each shoe, which is stiffened with cardboard so the doll can stand upright. Miss Korn-Krisp is 25" tall and has brown hair. The brand name is clearly visible in red letters across the front. Interestingly, this same doll was sold in 1899 to promote Cook's brand cereals under the names Miss Flaked Rice and Miss Malto-Rice.

Miss Korn-Krisp

The Sunny Jim doll sprang from an advertising blitz by the Force Food Co. of Buffalo, New York, to sell Force, its flaked wheat cereal. Humorous jingles about the life and

See Other Side
HOW TO GET A REGULAR SIZE
RAG DY-O-LA DYE DOLLY
TWELVE AND ONE HALF INCHES HIGH

Rag Dy-O-La Dye Dolly, circa 1912, with product name along the neckline

Sunny Jim postcards. The wagon card is postmarked 1902. Minnie Maud Hanff wrote the jingles for the advertising campaign; her high school friend Dorothy Ficken illustrated them.

2. *Unless otherwise noted, the remainder of the rag dolls discussed here are cut-and-sew advertising dolls."*

Jim Dumps' small
children liked to play
At "having parties" every day;
And so the merry
little brood
Had milk for tea
and "FORCE" for food.
"Twill keep the little folks
in trim;
What helpful play!" cried

Sunny Jim

A jingle about Jim and his children, from inside booklet

"The Story of Sunny Jim," booklet filled with jingles, circa 1902

habits of Sunny Jim and his cranky alter ego, Jim Dumps, were on billboards and inside streetcars all over the city. The first went like this:

> Jim Dumps was a most unfriendly man
> Who lived his life on the hermit plan.
> He'd never stop for a friendly smile,
> But trudged along in his moody style,
> 'Till "Force" one day was served to him—
> Since then they call him Sunny Jim.

and the second:

> Jim Dumps had tried some time in vain,
> To ease an after dinner pain
> Which gnawed at him his belt below
> And filled his world with indigo.
> Dyspepsia now can't bother him
> For "Force" has made him Sunny Jim.

Jim Dumps and Sunny Jim characters, "What To Buy and Where To Buy," January 1904

The Jim Dumps and Sunny Jim dolls came out in 1903, but the unfriendly Dumps was discontinued and is difficult for collectors to find today. Two trademarks from cereal packages, plus 4 cents in stamps, purchased one doll with full directions for cutting and sewing. The doll is linen, printed in five colors and 15" tall. Though there were minor variations in features or size, Sunny Jim continued to be offered for many years.

Sunny Jim doll, possibly 1940s

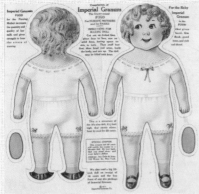

The miniature Imperial Granum doll

John Carle & Sons, maker of Imperial Granum, a food for nursing mothers and babies, offered a cloth doll at no cost in 1905. This 8" version is dated 1915. Orders were placed by writing the company or filling out a postcard. Twenty and 30" dolls were also available.

The Faultless Starch Co. of Kansas City, Missouri, advertised three different dolls in exchange for proof of purchase from boxes of starch. Six box tops and 10 cents in stamps for the return postage purchased Miss Elisabeth Ann, a 22" cloth doll. Twelve-inch dolls named Miss Phoebe Primm and Miss Lily White required three tops or fronts from the large box of starch or six from the small box and 4 cents in stamps for each doll. This uncut Phoebe Primm dates to 1912 and is stamped "The Saalfield Pub[lishing] Co., Akron, O."

A postcard with instructions for ordering the doll

Miss Phoebe Primm, 1912

In 1913 a Seattle, Washington, newspaper gave Anna Belle, Buster and Betsy dolls, "all ready to cut out, sew and stuff," with a new subscription. Anna Belle had "pretty golden hair and rosy cheeks" and stood 27" tall; Buster and Betsy measured 8" each. "Buster is a husky boy doll with a red striped sweater; Betsy is a little beauty and very loveable in her bright red coat. Both the little dollies are fully dressed ... Send us a new subscription to 'The Ranch' at 50 cents, and the names of three of your friends who you think would like to have a set of these dollies, and these three beautiful dollies—one big one and two smaller ones—will be sent you. Now in case you do not get a new subscription, just get your papa or mama to extend your own family subscription for one year."

Other newspapers in the area offered a Tango Rag Doll, with a different

Anna Belle, Buster and Betsy cut-and-sew dolls. The Ranch, Seattle, Washington. Oct. 1, 1913. "Chronicling America: Historic American Newspapers." Library of Congress.

face on each side, in exchange for a subscription. One side was named Mandy and the other Mabel, "all lithographed in glorious colors on strong, specially made muslin, 16x25 inches, with full printed directions, telling just how to cut out and stuff the dolls. Every youngster loves a doll—above all a rag doll made right at home. Drop it! Throw it!! Romp with it!!! Mandy and Mabel will not break. Take them with you to Slumberland." Mandy wore a bright yellow and green checked dress with a big yellow collar and red stockings. Mabel was dressed in vivid blue with black and yellow accents and matching blue stockings.

Heckers' Superlative Flour trade card, Hecker-Jones-Jewell Milling Co., 1894

Mandy and Mabel, the Tango Rag Doll. The Seattle (Washington) Star, April 11, 1914. "Chronicling America: Historic American Newspapers." Library of Congress.

Advertising dolls soon caught the attention of flour and grain millers. Since the mid-1890s, they had tucked free items into sacks, handed them out at point of purchase or made them available for a few cents by mail order. Ledgers, notebooks, pocket mirrors and lapel pins were given away with the grown-ups in mind. Storybooks, paper dolls, dollhouse furniture, coloring books and other paper items appealed to the children and brought Mom back to the store. Millers hoped the rag doll would, too.

The Forbes, Dutch and Russian dolls from Pillsbury's Best Flour paper dolls, Pillsbury-Washburn Flour Mills Co., July 30, 1895

Washburn's Gold Medal Flour doll furniture, "Other pieces of furniture will be found in other sacks of flour," Washburn Crosby Co., May 26, 1896

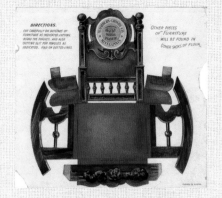

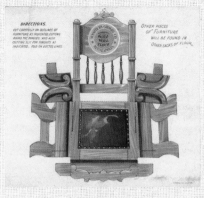

Washburn Crosby Co. mechanical trade card and paper doll, "One doll in each sack," 16 dolls to a set, circa 1896

"Quaker Nursery Rhymes," 1895, and "The Frolie Grasshopper Circus," 1898, children's booklets from the American Cereal Co. later known as Quaker Oats Co. The Frolie title, one of the finest advertising booklets of the 19th century, cost 2 cents to cover postage and was filled with colored pages of grasshoppers performing at the circus.

"White Fawn Drawing Book" from the George Young Bakery of Utica, New York, circa 1895-1897, a 3" x 3.75" booklet of pages to color or draw

Ralston-Purina Co. accordion booklet, circa 1903. Seven pages filled with rhymes and the cereal and activity for the day. "Thursday's the day you go to store, of Ralston-Purina Goods you'll want more. The dust that Friday's cleaning makes, is a task made easy if you eat Purina Pankakes ... "

This store poster reminded customers to save the coupons from Voigt's Crescent Flour to purchase a sleeping doll.

Bags of Worcester Salt contained coupons for various items on the company's premiums list. Six coupons purchased a set of 12 paper dolls; there were six different sets. Shown are a few of the dolls, an envelope that contained free ones and the Worcester Salt premiums list. Circa 1895-1910

Homeward bound with Bulte's Best,
Other cards will tell the rest—

Bulte's Best, so pure and white,
Cook receives it with delight.

Patty cake, patty cake fast as you can,
We hardly can wait 'til it's put in the pan.

Into the oven — now comes the test;
Soon we will show, 'twas Bulte's Best.

Out piping hot—just look at the size;
Surely these loaves would win first prize.

Of all the flour we've put to test
We'll use just one—that's Bulte's Best.

A series of six child-life postcards, advertised as "The Verdict,"
by Aug J. Bulte Milling Co., Kansas City, Missouri, 1909. The cost
for the set was 2 cents in stamps to cover postage.

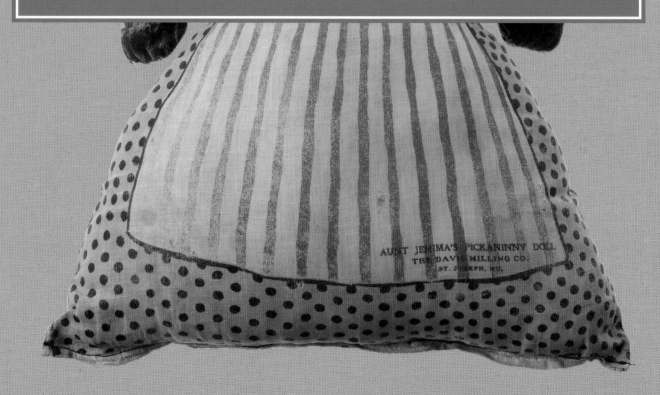

~ CHAPTER TWO ~
A MISSOURI FLOUR MILL AND
A FAMOUS RAG DOLL

*T*he Aunt Jemima doll is one of the most sought today and is believed to be the first cut-and-sew advertising doll offered by a flour miller. Its success as a toy had already been established when it was released in a set of six paper dolls. There was reason to think a cloth one would do just as well. It had to. The future of the newly reorganized Davis Milling Co. depended on it. A string of disasters had wreaked havoc on the company's predecessors and put its future in doubt. A rag doll, perhaps a family of them, could be just the thing to attract new customers and increase sales.

The story behind the dolls actually began in August 1888, when three men with widely different talents pooled their resources in a business venture in St. Joseph, Missouri. Newspaperman Christian L. Rutt, his brother-in-law William H. Wachtel and local attorney D.D. Burnes purchased an existing flour mill and incorporated it under the name Pearl Milling Co.

Wachtel had years of experience in the milling industry, and with Burnes' legal guidance and Rutt's stubborn tenacity, the mill was open for business less than seven weeks later. Sales were encouraging in the early months, so much so that they made news in a national milling periodical (right). Success was short-lived for the young company. A decline in demand for wheat flour in European markets contributed to a glut in the United States. Sales of ground cornmeal at home also began to slide as preferences leaned toward products sweetened with sugar. Fierce competition among mills caused sales to plummet, and Pearl Milling suffered along with the rest. Then, for reasons unknown, Wachtel left the company that year and assigned his shares to millworker Charles G. Underwood.

With their $4,000 investment at risk, the partners turned to a new idea to sell flour: a self-rising pancake mix that required only the addition of milk for a complete batter.[1] Rutt and Underwood spent months experimenting with

The Pearl Milling Co. has had its plant in operation only since Oct. 1 last, but in that time has won a large home and export trade. Its products are the "Pearl" meal, hominy, grits, graham flour, self-rising buckwheat, etc. They go largely to the south and also to Chicago and New York. The mill is on the roller process, with a thorough system of purification and degermination of the meal. The company is building up a large trade among western brewers with its germless meal, which is used in the place of rice for clarifying beer. —The Weekly Northwestern Miller, Feb. 8, 1889

---

[1] *The concept actually originated with another company that filed an application for patent on a "self-raising pan-cake flour" in 1876. The patent was granted to S.S. Marvin and Co. of Pittsburgh, Pennsylvania, on July 10, 1877. Advertisements for the mix explained, "Pan Cake Flour is just what its name implies, Flour for Pan Cakes, so prepared that the simple addition of cold water or sweet milk will make a batter from which delicious light cakes can be made instantly." The mix received special mention at the Pennsylvania State Fair at Erie in 1878 and was included in a display awarded a bronze medal. Visitors to the Pittsburgh Exposition in 1889 were served free pancakes and waffles made from Marvin's Pan Cake Flour. The company was purchased by National Biscuit Co. (Nabisco) about 1890 and continued to advertise the product in newspapers until at least January 1900.*

Rutt's recipe for Aunt Jemima pancake mix: 100 lbs. Hard Winter Wheat, 100 lbs. Corn Flour, 7 1/2 lbs. B.W.T. Phosphates from Provident Chem[ical], St. L[ouis], 2 3/4 lbs. Bicarb[onate] Soda and 3 lbs. Salt. Collection of Patee House Museum and Jesse James Home, St. Joseph, Missouri

ingredients before they felt confident enough to ask Purd Wright, the town librarian, to stop at Rutt's house and try a stack of pancakes. As his guest looked on, Rutt mixed and cooked the batter, drizzled the cakes with hot butter and syrup and handed the plate to Wright. The future of the company hung on the words of just one man who, years later, recounted the moment: "I ate the first perfected Aunt Jemima pancake and pronounced it good." Good was enough to satisfy all present. Packaging began and the mix soon appeared in local stores.

Expectations ran high but, unfortunately, the mix didn't sell. Rutt and Underwood had no real marketing plan and confined advertising and distribution to the local area. The name also posed a problem. Plain white paper bags marked Self-Rising Pancake Flour captured little attention and sat unsold on grocers' shelves. Then Rutt attended a theater performance in St. Joseph and had an idea from a character in the popular song, "Old Aunt Jemima." Why not rename the mix Aunt Jemima's Pancake Flour?

The first commercial use of the now famous name came on Nov. 27, 1889. Sadly, it was too late for sales to recover. With no operating cash and hope of attracting customers gone, the business collapsed. By the end of the year, Rutt returned to his job writing newspaper editorials and Underwood took a position with the R.T. Davis Mill Co. of St. Joseph. Details of what happened next are unclear, but it seems that Underwood and his brother Bert attempted to keep the pancake flour end of the business alive under the name Aunt Jemima Manufacturing Co. and applied for a trademark. The last-ditch efforts were in vain. In 1890, the R.T. Davis Mill Co. purchased Aunt Jemima Manufacturing Co., the recipe and the trademark.

THE R.T. DAVIS MILL
FINDS AUNT JEMIMA

Randolph True Davis was no newcomer to the flour business. He had more than 20 years of hard work invested in his mill, the largest in the area, and had built a fine reputation throughout the Missouri valley for selling quality products. He also had the funds necessary to improve and market the pancake flour and immediately set plans in motion. Corn sugar and rice flour were added to boost sweetness and texture. In what proved to be a brilliant decision, Davis next tried powdered sweet milk in the recipe and found the pancakes to be far superior to any made at home and in a fraction of the time. So convinced was he of the product, newspaper advertising began within the year for this first ever complete *instant* pancake mix. "Do you like hot pancakes in the morning?" "Aunt Jemima pancake flour for delicious cakes ready for instant use" and "To use it once is to use no other" were among early Aunt Jemima ads.

Even with advertising, sales remained low, and to complicate matters, a former business partner and local mill owner released his own brand of pancake mix. Newspaper advertisements for Aunt Sally's Pancake Flour ran right beside those of Aunt Jemima's and matched the price. If one dropped a half or even a quarter of a cent, so did the other.

Much to his credit, Davis understood where the real problem lay. It wasn't in the shelf price or the recipe itself but in the presentation. Somehow, the Aunt Jemima mix had to stand out as different. Customers needed to hear why they should buy it, and who better to tell them than a living, breathing representative of the name on the box.

Davis alerted food brokers to search the country for a natural actress with Southern charm and lots of personality, the perfect spokeswoman for pancakes. Wholesaler Charles Jackson notified Davis that he already knew the right woman for the job—the housekeeper for a friend in Chicago. Davis arranged a meeting and hired her on the spot.

Small-scale appearances in general merchandise stores were booked for her early on, but what Davis really wanted was a national stage to introduce this new face to the public. That stage turned out to be the Chicago World's Fair of 1893. Nancy Green, a 59-year-old former slave from Kentucky, stepped into the spotlight to play the role even better than Davis had imagined. From the company booth shaped like a giant flour barrel, she entertained the crowds with songs and stories of times long past, all the while demonstrating how

AUNT JEMIMA'S PAN CAKES.

Aunt Jemima offers a pancake sample to World's Fair visitors. Bismarck (North Dakota) Weekly Tribune, Aug. 18, 1893. "Chronicling America: Historic American Newspapers." Library of Congress.

Near the mills, for instance, is a mammoth barrel and an inscription thereon invites one to "Walk through and get an Aunt Jemima pancake free." I walked through, interviewed Aunt Jemima and got a pancake. It almost brought a tear to my eye. I could not think of eating the delicate, beautiful little thing. I had a silver dollar in my pocket, by chance. I placed it gently on the pancake and just enough of the yellow fringe showed around the border to make a fair model of an annular eclipse of the sun. The weight of the pancake was not quite one-fifth that of the dollar. But it was "free."

Reporter J. H. Beadle describes his pancake. Bismarck (North Dakota) Weekly Tribune, Aug. 18, 1893. "Chronicling America: Historic American Newspapers." Library of Congress.

easy it was to mix and cook the pancakes.[2] The invitation to "walk through and get an Aunt Jemima pancake free" was so effective that police had to be summoned to keep the crowds moving. Orders flooded in from around the world. By the end of the fair, Davis claimed to have received 50,000 orders for the mix. Green, named "Pancake Queen" by fair officials, received a lifelong contract.

Shortly after this, Purd Wright, the librarian taste-tester who now held the position of advertising manager for Davis Mill, authored a romanticized story about Nancy Green and titled the booklet "The Life of Aunt Jemima." It actually was a blend of some events from Green's life and a stereotypical version of a Civil War cook, ready to share her secret pancake recipe with Northerners and the rest of the world. Wright's story told what many people of the time wanted to hear. The booklet plus a lapel pin, also designed by Wright, engrained a smiling image of Aunt Jemima on the public.

Aunt Jemima lapel pin designed by Purd Wright, 1895

AUNT JEMIMA PAPER DOLLS

In 1895, the company tried a promotion aimed at children and already reported to be successful by millers, retailers and manufacturers across the country. For only 4 cents in stamps, Davis Mill mailed a set of six paper dolls: Aunt Jemima, Rastus and the four children: Abraham Lincoln, Delsie, Zeb and Dinah. Each doll came with an extra set of clothing to contrast the family's finances before and after the sale of the "receipt" (recipe). Older ones had a gift reserved with their interests in mind. "Send us your name and address and the name of your grocer and we'll send you a 40c sheet of music and words, 'Aunt Jemima's Lullaby.'" —The Kansas City Star, Jan. 30, 1897

---

[2] Their competitor, the R.W. Faucett Mill of St. Joseph, set up a log cabin at the Madison Square Garden Pure Food Exhibit in November 1895 to display Aunt Sally's Pancake Flour.

Reproduction of the R.T. Davis Mill Co.'s Aunt Jemima Before & After Receipt paper doll set, first sold in 1895. Collection of Arabella Grayson, writer/curator, "Two Hundred Years of Black Paper Dolls"

"Aunt Jemima's Lullaby," music by Samuel H. Speck, words by George Cooper

This advertisement offered the Aunt Jemima booklet and set of paper dolls for 4 cents in stamps.

"*Every bridge that spanned the Kansas river from Topeka to the mouth of the Kaw, except the Missouri Pacific Railroad bridge, which was weighted down by forty locomotives, was wrecked. Hundreds of homes were destroyed, business houses and factories wrecked, and other property damaged to an amount estimated at thirty-four million dollars in Kansas City, Kansas, and Kansas City, Missouri. Business was almost entirely suspended for a period of three months, while the thousands of people who had been driven from their homes, and the railroads, the manufactories and the great business concerns were righting things as best they could."*

R.T. Davis did not live to see the paper doll promotion. He died suddenly in December 1894. Shortly afterward, troubles befell the milling company. A severe depression crippled the country through much of the decade and brought unemployment topping 40 percent in some areas. Approximately one-fifth of the nation's railroad companies and 15,000 businesses went bankrupt, as did many of the banks that financed them. Conditions improved in 1898, and hopes were high for better times ahead.

Davis Mill reorganized in the spring of 1898 and consolidated the flour mill and Aunt Jemima Manufacturing Co., which until this time had operated as separate businesses. The newly formed R.T. Davis Mill & Manufacturing Co. had the backing of "$200,000 stock fully paid up," with all shares held by Davis' wife and two sons. The periodical "The Roller Mill" informed readers of the company's financial stability and explained the consolidation "insures a great increase in the volume of business." That may have been true for a while but, once again, changes were on the way.

In early May 1903, heavy rains began to fall in Missouri, Iowa, Kansas and Nebraska. The St. Joseph area sustained minimal damage from flooding, but the story was much different to the south. Kansas City was especially hard hit. The Kansas River became so swollen from rain that it filled valleys from bluff to bluff and measured an unimaginable five miles wide as it met the Missouri River in Kansas City. The book "History of Wyandotte County Kansas and Its People" describes the scene there during the first few days of June 1903 (left).

Eighteen years earlier, Davis Mill had established a branch house in the west bottoms of Kansas City. This branch was now completely submerged, along with 20 railroad cars holding almost 1 million pounds of flour. Flour the company desperately needed for sales lay ruined in water and muck. It was a hard blow for what the Kansas City Star described as "the pioneer milling firm of Northwest Missouri." R.T. Davis Mill & Manufacturing Co. declared bankruptcy on Sept. 1, 1903. Under the leadership of Robert R. Clark, the company reorganized the next year as Davis Milling Co., and again in February 1914 as Aunt Jemima Mills Co.

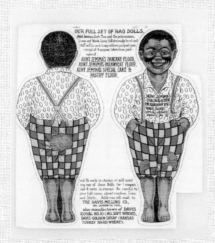

Wade Davis, stamped Davis Milling Company, 1909

First Aunt Jemima rag doll, 1905

Advertisement, Aunt Jemima Rag Doll Family, New York Tribune, Nov. 7, 1909. "Chronicling America: Historic American Newspapers." Library of Congress.

AUNT JEMIMA RAG DOLLS

Clark is credited with the rag doll promotion. An offer for "the famous Aunt Jemima in doll size—brightly colored and ready to cut out and stuff"—ran in newspapers during 1905. The doll wore a polka dot dress with a half apron stamped "The Davis Milling Co." and had a pretty kerchief tied around her hair. These early offers did not require proof of purchase but drew attention to the brand name by requesting return of the newspaper ad plus 6 cents in stamps. This changed the following year when a doll coupon was printed on the box of pancake flour. This coupon and two 2-cent stamps purchased one doll.

By 1909, advertisements included an entire family of rag dolls: Aunt Jemima, Uncle Mose and children Diana and Wade Davis. The interest was so great, more than 10 million had been purchased by 1921.

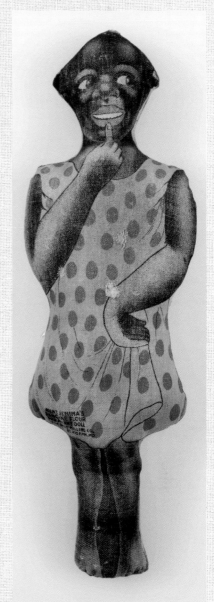

Diana Jemima, stamped Davis Milling Company, 1909

AUNT JEMIMA

RAG DOLL FAMILY
COUPON
SEE OTHER SIDE AS TO HOW TO SECURE THEM.

The Aunt Jemima family: Aunt Jemima, Uncle Mose, Wade Davis and Diana Jemima, 1914-1922, Aunt Jemima Mills Co.

A coupon for ordering the Aunt Jemima rag doll family, circa 1916

At least two more sets of cut-and-sew dolls were released by Aunt Jemima Mills before they were sold to the Quaker Oats Co. of Chicago in 1925-1926 for more than $4 million. Quaker Oats advertised the 1924 dolls until the supply was exhausted and then offered its own version in 1929. Two decades later, the company made one final change to the Rag Doll Family with an oilcloth version advertised as durable and washable. Demand lasted into the 1950s.

Aunt Jemima family, back

Diana Jemima flat panel, 1914-1922

A full-page ad for the Aunt Jemima Rag Doll Family, including coupon with ordering instructions, Aunt Jemima Mills Co., St. Joseph, "Woman's World," December 1916

Dolls in 1923 were brighter than previous ones.

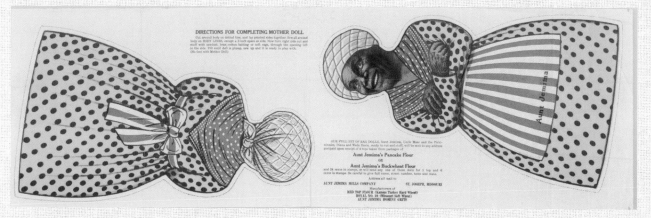

Aunt Jemima

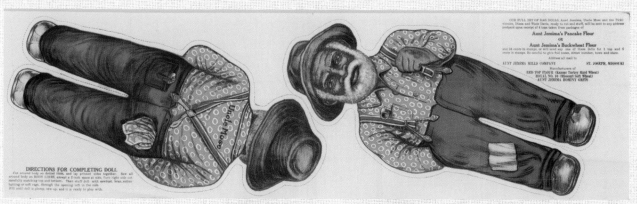

Uncle Mose

Wade "Aunt Jemima's Little Boy." Photo by Roger Nixon.

An uncut set from 1924.

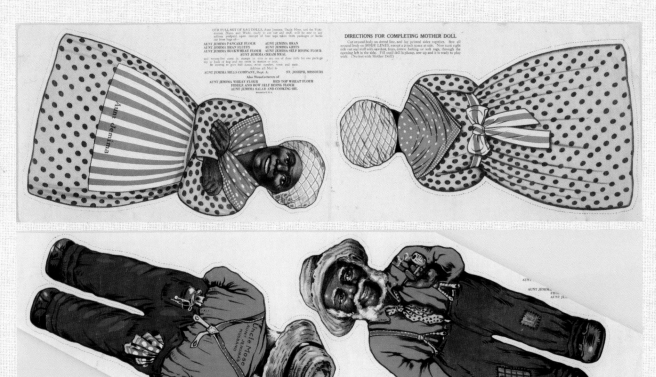

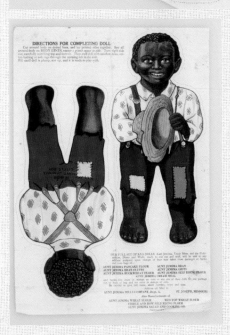

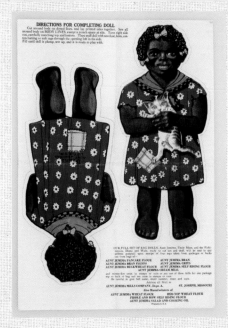

Aunt Jemima; Uncle Mose, "Aunt Jemima's husband"; Wade, "Aunt Jemima's Little Boy"; and Diana, "Aunt Jemima's Little Girl"

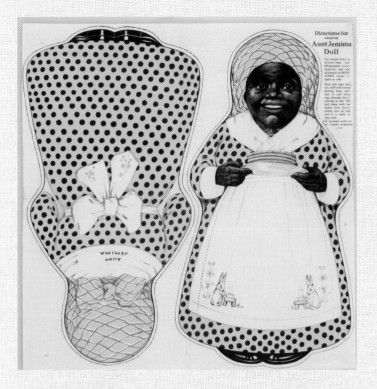

The decade ended with a new look for Aunt
Jemima, Quaker Oats Co., 1929

Wade, Quaker Oats Co., 1929,
Collection of Patee House
Museum and Jesse James
Home, St. Joseph, Missouri

Uncle Mose, Quaker Oats Co., 1929

THE DAVIS MILLING CO., ST. JOSEPH, MO., U. S. A.

Inexpensive items useful in the home were given away free, or for a few cents, with a box top from Aunt Jemima's Pancake Flour or other products in the line. Some of the more popular were postcards, needle books, recipe booklets, games, ink blotters and attractive cloth sacks.

This postcard shows the mill with an inset of Aunt Jemima and her famous, "I's in town Honey!" It was part of a souvenir postcard packet from 1908.

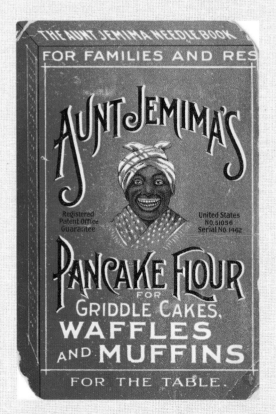

"The Aunt Jemima Needle Book," "A Household Necessity," by Davis Milling Co.. The interior has instructions for ordering the Rag Doll Family. Circa 1909

"Aunt Jemima's Special Cake & Pastry Flour," a die-cut recipe booklet by Davis Milling Co. It contains more than 30 numbered recipes and advertises a set of rag dolls. Circa 1906-1909

FIDDLE AND BOW RECIPES

FIDDLE AND BOW BISCUIT

Two cups (½ pint each) Fiddle and Bow Flour. Measure after sifting. Three tablespoonfuls of lard, 1 cup milk, enough to make soft dough. Knead only enough to roll out. Bake in quick oven.

STRAWBERRY SHORTCAKE

Two cups (½ pint each) Fiddle and Bow Flour. Measure after sifting. One-half cup sugar, three tablespoonfuls butter and lard mixed, one egg, milk enough to make soft dough. Bake in moderate oven. Cut in individual cakes after baking, split open and butter. Serve hot with fruit between and on top. The above will serve six people.

DOUGHNUTS

One cup sugar, three-fourths cup sour cream, three-fourths cup sweet milk, two eggs. Add enough Fiddle and Bow Flour to make a soft dough. Measure after sifting.

Insist on getting our products from your grocer. They are absolutely guaranteed by us to give satisfaction.

In recipes calling for baking powder, use Fiddle and Bow Flour. (Do not add baking powder or salt.)

Manufacturers

AUNT JEMIMA PANCAKE FLOUR
ROYAL No. 10 FLOUR
(Not Self Rising)
PLORAKO CREAM MEAL
BLUE D PEARL MEAL

AUNT JEMIMA MILLS COMPANY
ST. JOSEPH, MO.

Fiddle and Bow Ready Mixed Self Rising Flour needle book from Aunt Jemima Mills Co. Front cover and interior. Circa 1916

Aunt Jemima Pancake Flour ink blotter, 1920

The pretty patterned sacks that held Aunt Jemima flour were an added bonus to homemakers. This one dates to the 1950s.

~ CHAPTER THREE ~
DOLLS FROM FLOUR AND CEREAL MILLERS

*I*nterest in the Aunt Jemima dolls continued to build and made news in the article, "Little Girls' Plea for Doll Echoed Again."

"Please, I would like a papa doll, too."

These words written in a childish scrawl years ago started an idea that literally swamped the office of a great industrial plant.
Picture the president of a big manufacturing company sitting at his desk in the evening, after hours, doing up packages and sticking on stamps.

These are the high lights in the story of a famous family of rag dolls. Every mail brought in requests for them by the bushel basket. The very post-office authorities made inquiries to find out why they were sent out so slowly. Extra clerks were secured as rapidly as possible. But finally every employee—including the officers of the company—had to drop all the important affairs of a national milling business and concentrate on the one job of getting out rag dolls until the congestion was relieved ... —The Amarillo Globe, Dec. 29, 1924

Aunt Jemima was not alone. Other flour millers offered rag dolls in the early 20th century. One was printed right on the sack. Response was so high, it was used as a premium for about 10 years.

The Ceresota Boy Doll, cut and sewn from a printed cloth sheet, 1909. He stands about 15" tall. His boots are seamed down the center, with toes pointing forward.

CERESOTA AND DOLLY DIMPLE

Ceresota Boy Doll, back

The Northwestern Consolidated Milling Co. of Minneapolis, Minnesota, made a beautifully lithographed cut-and-sew doll available in 1909. To obtain it, the customer saved coupons found inside each sack or barrel of Ceresota Flour. It took the equivalent of one barrel of flour, or 198 pounds, to purchase a doll. Advertisements for the Ceresota Boy were few and usually consisted of a line or two placed in the newspaper by a store owner. "Use Ceresota Flour and enjoy good eating. Boy Doll Coupon in every sack. Sold by W.D. Hatch," The Holley Standard, New York, Sept. 23, 1909. Orders were submitted directly to the milling company.

Coupons with instructions for ordering the Ceresota Boy Doll. "These coupons are packed in every sack and barrel of Ceresota Flour, on the basis of 16 to the barrel."

Rare, uncut panel, second version of the Ceresota Boy Doll with boots pointed to each side, 1909

16 BLACK COUPONS, when sent to The Northwestern Consolidated Milling Co., entitles the sender to one cloth **Ceresota Boy Doll,** by mail, FREE.

Or 8 GREEN COUPONS, when sent to The Northwestern Consolidated Milling Co., entitles the sender to one cloth **Ceresota Boy Doll,** by mail, FREE.

Or 4 ORANGE COUPONS, when sent to The Northwestern Consolidated Milling Co., entitles the sender to one cloth **Ceresota Boy Doll,** by mail, FREE.

Or 2 BLUE COUPONS, when sent to The Northwestern Consolidated Milling Co., entitles the sender to one cloth **Ceresota Boy Doll,** by mail, FREE.

Or 1 RED COUPON, when sent to The Northwestern Consolidated Milling Co., entitles the sender to one cloth **Ceresota Boy Doll,** by mail, FREE.

These coupons are packed in every sack and barrel of **Ceresota Flour,** on the basis of 16 to the barrel. Write name and address plainly and mail to

COUPON DEPARTMENT
THE NORTHWESTERN CONSOLIDATED MILLING CO.
MINNEAPOLIS, MINN.

Coupon back

In 1912, Northwestern Consolidated Milling published an activity book for children called "The Adventures of Ceresota: A Painting Book in Story Form." Stories, color charts and 12 pages to paint were enough to keep young fingers busy for an afternoon. The book sold for 10 cents and included a set of Japanese watercolors in red, yellow and blue.

A rare piece of ephemera is "Ye Old Style Wind Mill" from the company's first year in business. The card is dated May 10, 1892. The Ceresota Cook Book with a string hanger is much easier to find.

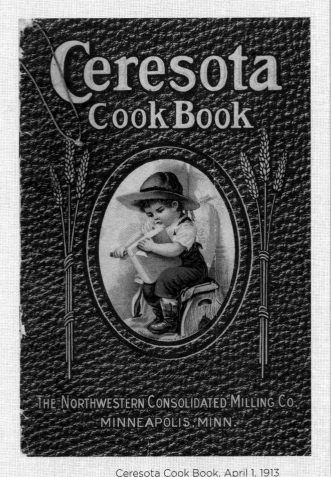

"The Adventures of Ceresota: A Painting Book in Story Form," 1912, with Japanese watercolor sheets

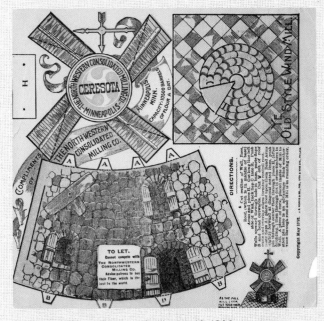

Ceresota Flour paper windmill, May 10, 1892

"The Adventures of Ceresota," Illustration #7

Ceresota Cook Book, April 1, 1913

An uncut Dolly Dimple Flour sack in blue, stamped "Copyrighted by Arkadelphia Milling Co. 1914, Patented March 9, 1915 Serial Number 866869." Fulton Bag and Cotton Mills of St. Louis made the sack.

Doll back. The directions for cutting and sewing suggested that cardboard be added to the shoe soles.

Dolly Dimple Flour doll, about 18" tall, dressed in lace-trimmed undergarments, available from 1914 to about 1924

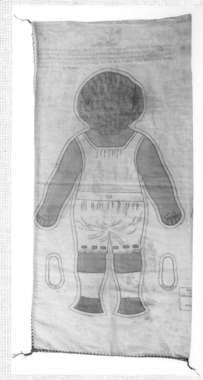

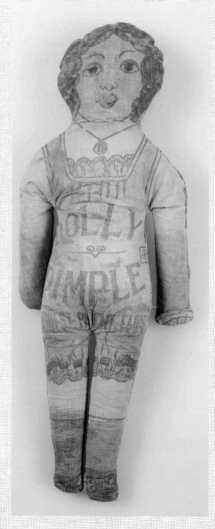

The Dolly Dimple Flour doll became available shortly before World War I broke out in 1914 and has the distinction of being the first doll printed directly on a flour sack. She came in red or blue, depending on the type of flour purchased. Eight years after release, the Dolly Dimple doll remained immensely popular and was the subject of an article, "Getting the Consumer to Use the Container." It said, in part,

"A container which the buyer can make use of after the contents have been consumed has often proved a powerful stimulant for reorders. Makers of novelties, perfumers, confectioners and milliners have made use of this idea to great advantage. The Cinco tin cigar box with a handy catch which the man can use as a container for pen points, fish hooks, cigar coupons and similar odds and ends was an adaptation of the novelty man's idea. It is rather more unusual to find the manufacturer of a staple like flour using a similar plan.

The Arkadelphia Milling Co. of the city by that name in Arkansas is maker of Dolly Dimple Self-Rising Flour. The flour is contained in a patented cambric sack with one-half of a large pattern of a doll on each side. Full directions for making a real cambric doll are printed on each sack at one side of the doll, and on the other are the directions for using the flour to make biscuits. The sack is featured in this firm's advertising and as there is something about the design which appeals to the mother's heart as well as the child's, it has caused many sales and reorders." —Printers' Ink, Dec. 28, 1922

Advertisement, Hattiesburg American, Oct. 11, 1921

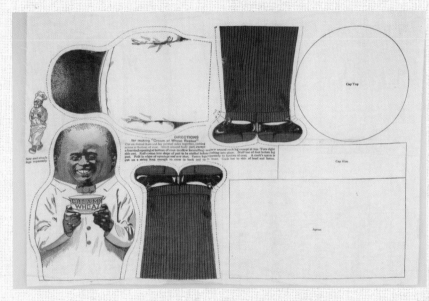

Cream of Wheat Rastus doll, circa 1925-1940, approximately 18" tall

CEREAL MILLERS JOIN THE FUN

The 1920s ushered in prosperity for businesses across the country. Advances in technology and improvements in the quality of consumer goods brought customers out in full force. Advertising budgets swelled, which meant more money for ads in newspapers and magazines.

Cereal millers used advertising to introduce new brands, strengthen sales of established ones or offer premiums. The Cream of Wheat Co. hired prominent artists to create magazine and billboard ads, including J.C. Leyendecker, famous for his covers on "Saturday Evening Post," and Jessie Willcox Smith, the illustrator of "Heidi," "Little Women" and "An Old Fashioned Girl." In the

Dolly Dimple in red

Flat panel for Daddy Bear

first half of the 1920s, the company introduced a cut-and-sew doll named "Cream of Wheat Rastus." Later versions call him the "Cream of Wheat Chef Doll." Popularity was so high, the doll was given as a premium for about 30 years.

In 1926, the Kellogg Co. of Battle Creek, Michigan, advertised a set of dolls based on a beloved children's story. "Send for Goldilocks and the Three Bears.

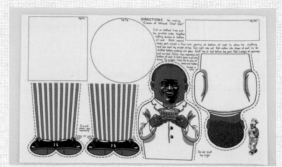

Cream of Wheat Chef Doll, circa 1940s

Children love these beautiful cloth dolls. 12" to 15" tall—lithographed in six colors. 10c and the top of a Kellogg's Corn Flakes package will bring any one of these dolls. Four such tops and 30c for all four."

An even more spectacular set from Kellogg's called the Nursery Rhyme or Fairyland dolls debuted in 1928. Each cloth sheet carried a bonus of two leaves from a book. When all four dolls had been collected, the leaves could be sewn together to make a miniature nursery

Kellogg's Daddy Bear, Mama Bear, Johnny Bear and Goldilocks

rhyme book. The characters available for order were Little Bo Peep, Mary and Her Little Lamb, Tom the Piper's Son and Little Red Riding Hood. The price was the same as the Goldilocks set, with participating cereals listed as Corn Flakes, Rice Krispies, Pep, All-Bran, Shredded Wheat Biscuit, Krumbles and even Kellogg's own Kaffee Hag coffee.

Mary and Her Little Lamb

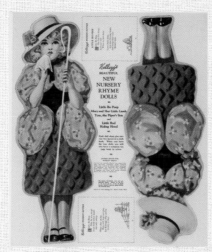

Little Bo Peep

Tom the Piper's Son

Kellogg's dolls reverse side

Fairy tale and nursery rhyme booklets from flour and cereal millers: "Mother Hubbard and the Fairies," 1927, Hubbard Milling Co.; "The Story of Miss Pokodot and the Dwarfies," 1923, Pokodot Cereal Co.; "Hob O' the Mill," 1927, and "Around the World With Hob," 1930, Quaker Oats Co.; "Mother Goose and Her Goslings," 1919, Knapp Co. Inc., for Wells-Abbott-Nieman Co.

Fairies and tales about them fascinated children of the 1920s. Millers took note and used them to advertise. Fairies appeared on the front of cereal boxes, in brightly colored advertisements and on premiums. Quaker Oats' plan to use them in a campaign for its new breakfast cereal made news in the Aug. 19, 1920, issue of *Printers' Ink:*

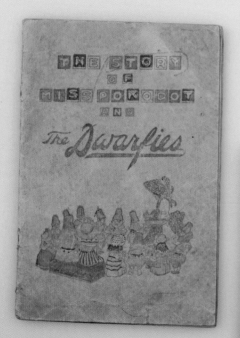

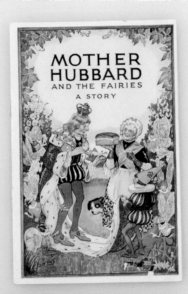

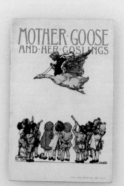

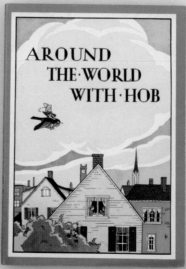

"Children are rapidly coming into their own as recognized factors in the great scheme of buying. Time was when their influence in deciding purchases for the home was overlooked or minimized. But now we see a big national advertising campaign in which the whole consumer appeal is directed to children alone …

The Quaker Quakies copy which has just started in national mediums is along the fairy-tale order. Right here we see some good advertising psychology. A fairy tale appeals to almost anybody with imagination. It is said that President McKinley when tired and worried over the hard problems of his office would find refuge and rest in reading books like Alice in Wonderland. Most people will read a fairy story if it is short enough and if they think they won't get caught at it. Yet if advertising of this kind were addressed to grown-ups they would think it beneath their dignity and have little respect for the article advertised.

On the other hand, address the thing to the children and the grown-ups will read it. They will smile tolerantly and then call little Willie and Mary, show them the attractive picture and read them the pretty story. The net result is they have driven in upon them in a forceful way the fact that there is a new breakfast food on the market named Quaker Quakies, which of course is just what the advertiser is trying to bring about. All this is done in recognition of the principle of utilizing imagination in advertising and in allowing the powerful indirect appeal to do its work."

THE TOOTH FAIRY VISITS A FLOUR MILL

Larabee Flour Mills used a fairy story to appeal to children and chose one that was gaining wide acceptance in this country—the tooth fairy.

The tooth fairy had its origin centuries ago. During the Middle Ages, a child in England was taught to drop a baby tooth into the fire or spend the afterlife searching for it. Warriors in northern Europe thought it good luck to wear a necklace made from children's teeth into battle and paid a fee to obtain them. In some Middle Eastern countries, a baby tooth was thrown toward the sun with a request that a better one replace it. In Asian countries, the tooth could be thrown onto the roof, on the ground, into the space beneath the floor or simply into the air.

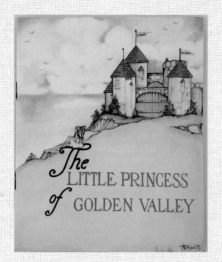

"The Little Princess of Golden Valley" book

Although difficult to pinpoint with certainty, the tooth fairy's appearance in this country appears to date to the early 1900s. A 1908 newspaper article titled "Tooth Fairy" explains the story much as it is told today:

"Many a refractory child will allow a loose tooth to be removed if he knows about the tooth fairy. If he takes his little tooth and puts it under the pillow when he goes to bed the tooth fairy will come in the night and take it away, and in its place will leave some little gift. It is a nice plan for mothers to visit the 5 cent counter and lay in a supply of articles to be used on such occasions." —Omaha Daily Bee, Oct. 5, 1908

The story gained acceptance during the 1920s and by the second half of the decade, Esther Watkins Arnold had written a short play on the subject.[1] Two years later, Larabee Flour Mills Co. of Kansas City offered customers a unique castle and paper doll set based on its version of the story. Larabee called it "The Little Princess of Golden Valley" and began it this way:

[1] *A lone copy of "The Tooth Fairy: Three Act Playlet for Children," 1927, is held at Brown University Library in Providence, Rhode Island.*

Little Princess cut-outs

"Do you know that a Little Princess lives right here in your own country? Perhaps you don't know that, but it is true. She lives in a castle with towers and bridges and everything that Little Princesses had in castles long ago. Our Little Princess' castle stands on a hillside overlooking a wonderful valley where the sun shines so much it is called the 'Golden Valley.'

The Little Princess would be very happy but for one thing—she loves children so much that she wants all of them to be well and strong, and she knows that they cannot be well and happy unless their enemies are beaten. It makes her sad to know that enemies are all around. Those enemies would harm little children were it not for the Little Princess, who spends her time protecting their health and happiness.

On one side of the Golden Valley is a country with a long, long name—Malnutrition. These ugly people are bitter enemies …

… Now, the Little Princess is brave and she is wise, too! She will not let these enemies harm happy children. Not if she can help it. And she can—because she has an army of her own—and the army is found right in the Golden Valley.

The army stands ready to keep the enemy away. Good Knight Sir Larabee is always ready to fight the children's battles. And there are the Fairies and Elves. They do not fight, but, like all regular armies, they form the supply department. The little Elves slide down into the valley on sunbeams; their suits are made of pieces of that blue, blue sky. And the Fairies come a-riding on the rain, their lovely dresses all colors of the rainbow, for that's where they come from—the rainbow itself.

Down into the valley come the raindrops and sunbeams. There is work to be done … "

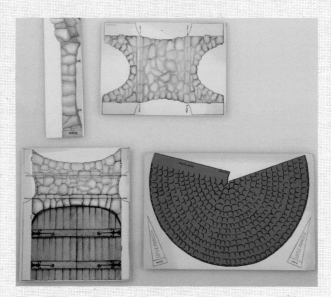

Turret Bridges

Underweight

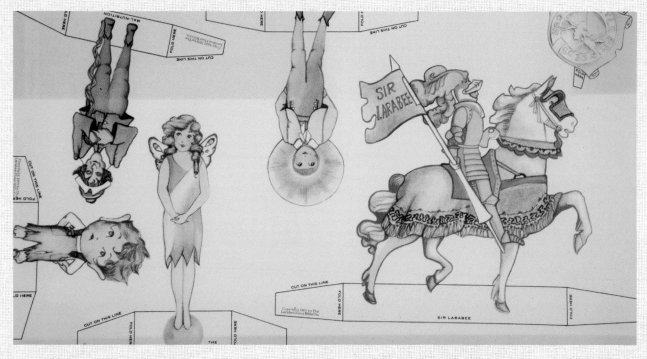

Sir Larabee and others

Larabee Flour Mills continued the fairy theme 20 years later on these dress print sacks of Airy Fairy Flour. The sacks were made by the Percy Kent Bag Co. Collection of Edie McGinnis

The story has a happy ending. The good army wins the battle against Malnutrition, Underweight and other enemies of children's health, and the children are reminded to "think of all the good things Mother can make for you with Little Princess Flour. Surely *you* will live 'happily ever after.' Now—won't you?"

Newspaper ads in *The Kansas City Star* explained that a "coupon in each package tells how to build a complete castle." "Tell Mother to be sure and buy Little Princess Flour. The carton looks just like a castle. What fun you can have playing with the castles and the Little Princess cut-outs, drawbridges, etc. Get the interesting story book, Little Princess of Golden Valley."—Jan. 20, 1929

Two sets were available. The first contained the storybook, turret, bridges and two cut-outs of the Little Princess. Ten character cut-outs came in the second set. An instruction sheet reminded children to save the empty round cartons of flour for the turrets. "The more turrets you have, the more fun."

Jenny Germ and others

RODKEY MILLING AND THE RAG DARLINGS

The next series of flour dolls came out of the dark days of the Great Depression and from one of the hardest-hit areas in the country: Oklahoma.

The Rodkey family of Edmond, Oklahoma, is credited for a quality doll named Rag Darling that was printed on sacks of flour from their mill.

Their story began in 1897, when Isaac and Catherine Rodkey moved to Edmond to purchase a 50 percent share in an existing flour mill. Isaac had prepared well for the business, spending most of the 1880s studying flour milling in McPherson, Kansas. It was there he met and married Alice Kate (known as Catherine) Rank. Two children, Bess and Earl, soon followed and were joined by a brother, Don, shortly after the family settled in Edmond.

The mill, renamed Eagle Milling Co., prospered under the leadership of Rodkey and partner George Farrar. Duties were evenly divided. Farrar managed the office and bookkeeping; Rodkey alternated travel to secure new flour sales with the grinding and shipping activities back at the mill. In the early years, the company sold grain, coal, feed and two brands of flour. Carloads of Gilt Edge and White Frost flour left Edmond on the Santa Fe Railway for general stores throughout Oklahoma and Texas. Business boomed. By spring 1906, Eagle Milling began extensive improvements and closed for about a month. When it reopened, capacity had increased 25 percent. Business continued to grow enough that when Farrar left the company in 1914, Rodkey bought him out and offered the share to his son, Earl. Don joined the family business in 1920.

Rag Darling flyer and mailer

Catherine was happy in Edmond, too, and thrived in the social activities of city life. She founded the Edmond Gardening Club and was responsible for much of the landscaping in the city parks. She also enjoyed entertaining and was known throughout the area as a fine hostess. Many of her parties made the news, as this one did in 1903:

"A reception carrying out the rose idea was the social event of last week, when Mesdames J.W. Howard, I.W. Rodkey and G.B. Farrar entertained over sixty ladies last Thursday afternoon at the home of Mrs. Rodkey. The house was beautifully decorated with roses. In one corner, on a solid bank of roses was the punch bowl, and in it too (sic) very perfect large red roses rested on a cake of ice. The punch bowl was charmingly presided over by Miss Mae Thatcher. Refreshments were served and in this too the rose idea was carried out as the ice cream had been moulded into the shape of roses and was of a rose color. The menu was cream chicken with mushrooms, sandwiches, pickle and coffee, and ice cream and cakes ... "—Edmond Enterprise and Oklahoma County News, May 21, 1903

In December 1934, during the depths of the Great Depression when every penny counted, Eagle Milling[1] printed the first in a series of brightly colored dolls on its sacks of Rag Darling Flour. General stores received posters to place in their windows. Flyers and mailers were readied for store owners, salesmen, jobbers and anyone who could not be contacted in person. A portion of the sales presentation explained:

"Rag Darling has an irresistible appeal to children. The quality of Rag Darling Flour has an irresistible appeal to the cook. It is a repeater. Your customers will want dolls in every one of the sizes. A constant reminder of Rag Darling Flour ...

Rag Darling is life-like, natural, attractive. Mothers can complete this doll through simple directions by sewing and stuffing."

---

[1] Later known as Rodkey Flour Mill

The first Rag Darling doll, about 21" tall before stuffing, on a 48-pound sack made by the Bemis Bag Co.

The first Rag Darling doll, reminiscent of the refined and elegant Catherine, wore a lovely striped dress, accented with bright red bows at the waist and shoulders, a pearl necklace and a matching hair bow. The rest of the dolls came in a rainbow of colors—purple, blue, yellow, red and green—with a single large bow at the neck and another in the hair. Dolls were available on 3-, 6-, 12-, 24- and 48-pound sacks.

Purple Rag Darling doll, approximately 11" tall, 6-pound sack

Blue, 6 pounds

Yellow, 48 pounds. The sack was made by the Percy Kent Bag Co. and stamped, "This is not the ordinary flour bag. It is the highest quality cambric."

Red, 6 pounds. A small gold paper label shaped like a bag of flour is attached to both sides of the sack. This may be an extension of the advertising used for the Gilt Edge brand flour, which said, "Avoid substitutes. Look for gold medals on every sack."

Green, a mere 7" tall, 3-pound sack

Advertising poster, red doll

A sack of Rodkey's Best Flour with a logo almost as pretty as the dolls. The brand was added to the company's line of products around the 1910s.

At least two advertising posters were used. Children who passed a store with a sign in the window were sure to see the doll and beg their parents to stop and buy it.

A grain elevator and office are the only structures remaining from Rodkey Flour Mill. The doll and flour sacks filled there are collector's items today and a cherished part of Edmond history.

FLOUR SACK DOLLS OF THE 1930S AND '40S

Popularity for the flour sack doll peaked during the 1930s and 1940s. As the Great Depression tightened its grip on the country, a free doll printed on a sack became a strong draw. It might be the only toy a child had and meant precious funds saved for the family. The cotton shortages of World War II also contributed to high demand for the dolls. Many were not advertised by name but simply called "cut outs" in newspaper and grocery ads. Little if any history can be found for most of them. Mills kept meticulous records on the flour, daily output, lab analysis reports and the like but rarely made note of the dolls. Some are surprised today when they hear of the dolls that once came from their own mills.

W. Lee O'Daniel's Hillbilly Patty Boy, circa 1938

Front: Hillbilly Flour, W. Lee O'Daniel Flour Co., Fort Worth, Texas. Fulton Bag Co. made the sack. The flour was milled at Wichita Mill & Elevator Company, Wichita Falls, Texas.

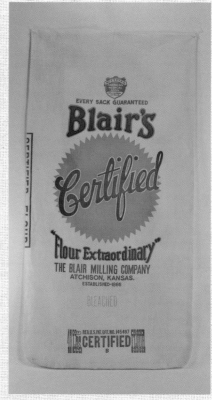

Pokey the Pony was printed on the back of this sack from Obelisk Self-Rising Flour, Ballard & Ballard Co. Inc., Louisville, Kentucky. Werthan Bag Co. made the sack.

Certified Pig Doll. Instructions say, "Cut along dotted line, sew together leaving small opening for stuffing. Then complete the sewing and you have a Certified Pig Doll." Collection of Donna di Natale

Front: Blair's Certified Flour, Blair Milling Co., Atchison, Kansas. Chase Bag Co. made the sack. Collection of Donna di Natale

Unnamed Bunny Doll, Victor Flour, stamped "Copyrighted 1935, The Crete Mills, Crete, Nebraska." Bemis Bag Co. made the sack.

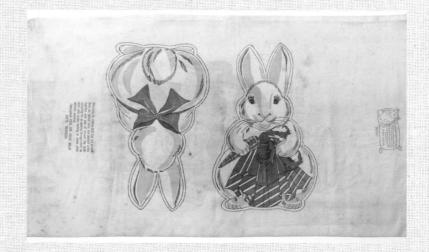

Front: Peerless Flour, Peerless Flour Mills Co., Norton, Kansas. Made by Bemis Bag Co.

Unnamed doll

Crete Mills advertised a 25" x 29" Puppet Doll Stage to customers of Victor Flour in November 1937.

"Boys! Girls! Grown-ups! There is entertainment, fun, excitement galore waiting for every user of Victor Flour! Now, you can own one of these thrilling Puppet Doll Shows that will bring hours of amusement to every member of the family! Pogo, Sassafras, Jimmie and Alice are printed on the backs of the Victor Flour sacks, waiting for you to put them together—to make them sing, dance, play and act just like real live actors.

Inside of each sack of Victor Flour, you'll find full information how you can get your complete outfit including a large stage, backdrop, curtain, full-length playlet and all instructions so you can start right in giving shows just like a professional puppeteer. Give them at home for fun—give them for church or school benefits! Get your Victor Flour now and be the first in your neighborhood to have your Victor Puppet Doll Show!"

Mitchell Daily Republic, November 11, 1937. Photo courtesy of Korrie Wenzel, Publisher, *The Daily Republic*

Front: Victor Flour, Crete Mills, Crete, Nebraska. Bemis Bag Co. made the sack. This one is advertised as percale. Some were printed on coarse muslin.

Unnamed Sunflower Doll, Bewley's Best Flour, Bewley Mills, Ft. Worth, Texas

Pogo and Alice, 1937

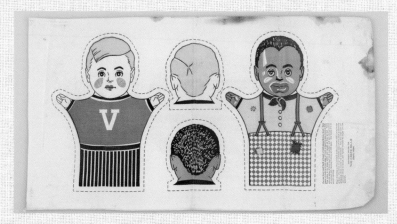

Jimmie and Sassafras, Victor Flour, Crete Mills, 1937

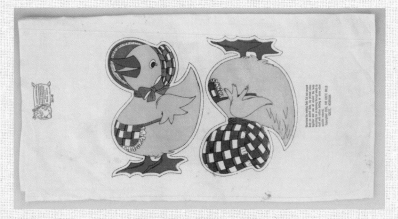

Unnamed characters, probably Humpty Dumpty (right) and Mother Goose (above), Victor Flour, Crete Mills, 1935. Collection of Edie McGinnis.

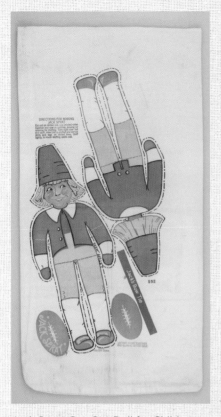

Jack Sprat Cut-Out Doll for Children

Front: Jack Sprat Flour, Jack Sprat
Foods Inc., Marshalltown, Iowa.
Percy Kent Bag Co. made it.

"Bewley's Traffic Cop," Bewley's
Best Flour, not dated

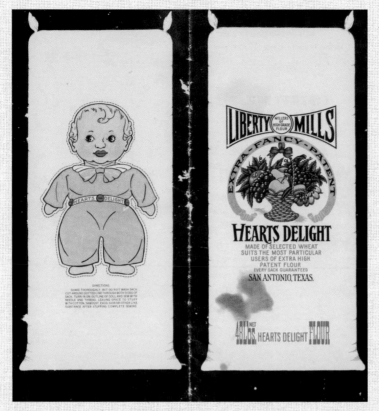

Hearts Delight Doll and booklet of sewing instructions for a complete nursery set using the doll cut-outs found on Hearts Delight Flour, Liberty Mills, San Antonio, Texas

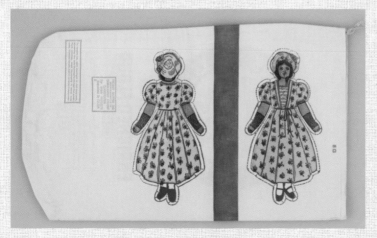

Unnamed Bewley's Doll, 10 pounds, Bewley's Best Flour, 1947

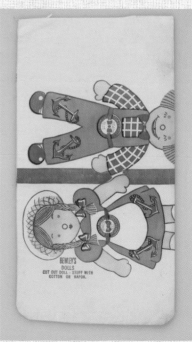

Unnamed "Bewley's Dolls," 12 pounds, Bewley's Best Flour, 1941

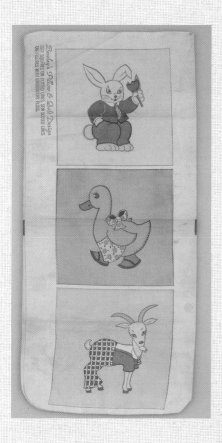

Bewley Mills packed flour in bags with pillow and quilt designs made especially for young customers. Some blocks were complete and needed only to be sewn together. Others required a bit of embroidery.

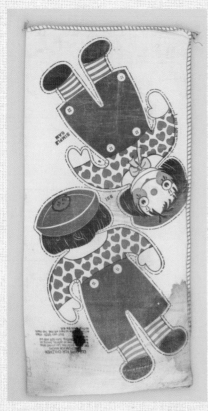

Simple Sam

Front: Little King Flour, Colonial Flour Co., Little Rock Arkansas. The sack was made by Percy Kent Bag Co. and was closed with a pretty mauve thread.

Miss Supreme Sugar, Supreme Sugar Co. Inc., Baton Rouge, Louisiana

Puppet Doll, Little King Flour

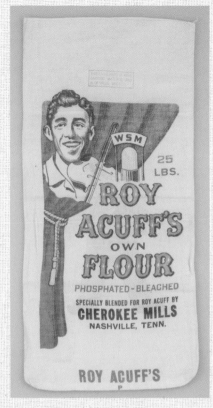

The doll on this 25-pound flour sack was named after country music star Roy Acuff. Circa 1944-1947.

Front: Roy Acuff's Own Flour by Cherokee Mills, Nashville, Tennessee

Kiddy Kut-Outs, unnamed dolls, Millhiser Bag Co., Richmond, Virginia. The front of the sack is blank.

Don the Day and Night Doll, Our Best Flour, Greeneville Milling Co.

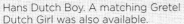
Hans Dutch Boy. A matching Gretel Dutch Girl was also available.

Front: Our Best Flour, Greeneville Milling Co., Greeneville, Tennessee. The sack is stamped "Educational Cut-Outs" and was made by Werthan Bag Co. for the "6-way Nourishment" educational campaign sponsored by leading flour millers and the Wheat Flour Institute of Chicago from 1948 to 1950.

Don in softer colors of pink and slate blue

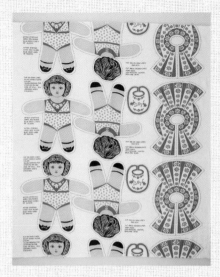

Betty Bemis, Bemis Bro. Bag
Co., St. Louis, Missouri

Teddy Bear, Bemis Bro. Bag Co.

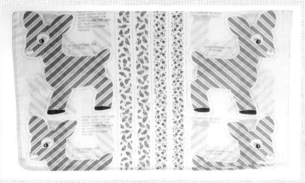

Phil Fawn, Bemis Bro. Bag Co.

New York artists designed Betty Bemis, Phil Fawn
and Teddy Bear for the Bemis Bag Co. in the late 1940s.
"Bemis Cut-outs will be in demand by the pigtail set. The
kids will see to it that Mamma buys the feed in the Bemis
bag with the cut-outs ... dolls with doll clothes for the
toddlers, teddy bears and cute fawns for the older ones."
—"The Feed Bag," November 1949

Seymour Airplane Factory,
Voigt Flour, Voigt Milling Co.,
Grand Rapids, Michigan

Toy bank with key, Hillbilly
Flour, W. Lee O'Daniel Flour
Co., Fort Worth, Texas

Older boys and girls were not left out. Flour mills offered specialty items to appeal to them. Victor Flour had an All-American Football Game, and Robin Hood Flour offered an archery set. In the late 1920s, Voigt Milling promoted interest in aviation with a construction set called the Seymour Airplane Factory. It sold for $1.69. The O'Daniel Flour Co. gave away toy banks in the shape of a flour barrel at political rallies for owner W. Lee O'Daniel. Kasco Mills published two comic books, and Bay State-Wingold gave train and truck cut-outs.

Cut-outs, Bay State-Wingold Flour, Bay State Milling Co., Winona, Minnesota

Kasco Komics No. 2, 1949,
Kasco Mills Inc., Toledo, Ohio

TWO SPECIAL QUAKER OATS DOLLS

Quaker Oats had its start in 1877, when the Quaker Mill Co. of Ravenna, Ohio, registered the first trademark for a breakfast cereal. The Quaker name was chosen "as a symbol of good quality and honest value." More than 20 years of mergers among oat and cereal mills followed before the company known as the Quaker Oats Co. emerged in 1901.

A memorable event in the company's history occurred during the St. Louis World's Fair in 1904. Botanist Alexander P. Anderson, already partnered with Quaker to work on his theory of puffed rice, set up a demonstration booth where he loaded eight short, cannon-like cylinders with raw rice. The cylinders were then capped and heated to 572 degrees Fahrenheit. As each cap was removed, a volley of hot, puffed rice shot out and into a special wire cage. Female attendants fanned out into the audience to offer sample bags of the "new confection" for 5 cents each. By the end of the fair, 250,000 bags had been sold. Quaker Oats added Puffed Rice and Puffed Wheat to its cereal line and called them "The Eighth Wonder of the World" and "Food Shot From Guns."

Puffy the Quaker Oats doll debuted in 1930. He was about 16 1/2" tall and carried boxes of Puffed Wheat and Puffed Rice. An advertisement on the cloth sheet said the cereals were "shot from huge guns."

During the golden age of radio, Quaker advertised Crackels cereal, "crisp little golden pillows that look like confections," on its 15-minute program for children hosted by popular radio personality Phil Cook. He played the ukulele, sang, told funny stories and advertised Quaker Oats products, including this Crackels doll. Crackels is dated 1930 and measures about 16 1/2" tall.

"The Eighth Wonder of the World," Quaker Puffed Rice postcard, 1905

Puffy, 1930

Phil Cook advertising the Quaker Crackels doll

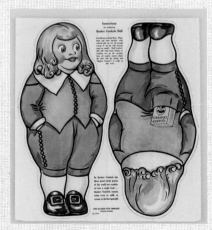

Crackels, 1930

A booklet for children from Phil Cook's radio show. "Simple Simon's School House: Attention Poopils!" by Quaker Oats for Aunt Jemima Pancake Flour, circa 1930.

MORE KELLOGG'S, PLEASE

W.K. Kellogg, founder of the Kellogg Co., made an unheard of move to put folks in Battle Creek, Michigan, back to work during the Great Depression. While many other businesses were cutting back on hours, Kellogg did the opposite. Effective Dec. 1, 1930, he reduced the workday of the plant's three shifts from eight to six hours and then gave employees a pay raise. A fourth shift was created specifically for the unemployed. Positions opened for landscapers and gardeners in the company's 10-acre park on the Battle Creek plant grounds. Kellogg's promise, "I'll invest my money in people," became a reality, and employee morale soared.

Kellogg doubled the advertising budget that year, and customers responded. Cereal sales and profits increased, which led to more advertising. The use of premiums resumed.

In 1931, the Kellogg Co. sponsored Irene Wicker as "The Singing Lady," the first radio network program for children. An advertising premium to acquaint parents and children with the program said: "The Singing Lady tells the stories dear to childhood; sings the most delightful songs. She keeps youngsters breathless and eager at the radio." Kellogg printed

Paper dolls to promote Kellogg's radio program, 1932. "The Singing Lady tells the stories dear to childhood; sings the most delightful songs. She keeps youngsters breathless and eager at the radio."

several booklets for young listeners. This one from 1933, "Mother Goose: As Told by Kellogg's Singing Lady," required one box top from any Kellogg cereal and 10 cents.

A parade of colorful dolls awaited Kellogg's customers from the mid-1930s to the late 1940s. Four cereal package tops and 25 cents purchased: Crinkle the Cat, Dinkey the Dog, Freckles the Frog and Dandy the Duck in 1935. One doll cost 10 cents and one box top.

Mother Goose Singing Lady booklet and coupon for ordering, 1933

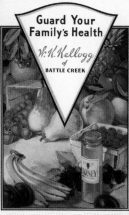

Kellogg paper dolls, undated, circa 1930s

Kellogg's first premium was directed to children. Funny Jungleland Moving Pictures, filled with animal pictures and short rhymes, 1909

Crinkle the Cat and companions, Oct. 14, 1935

Dinkey the Dog

Dandy the Duck

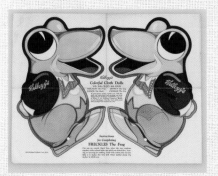

Freckles the Frog

Snap

Crackle

Pop

Kellie the Dog

Chiquita Banana Doll

Snap, Crackle and Pop dolls arrived in 1948 and brought a slight price increase to 15 cents each. Kellie the Dog from Kellogg's Gro-Pup dog food came out the same year.

This first release of the Chiquita Banana Doll is dated 1949 and was followed by several other versions.

HONORABLE MENTION

Little Crow Foods of Warsaw, Indiana, had its start in 1903 as a flour mill. Pancake flour was added to the product line in 1919, followed by CoCo Wheats hot cereal in the opening months of the Great Depression. As the 1940s drew to a close, Little Crow ran advertisements for a doll on the back of its cereal and muffin mix boxes. One box top and 25 cents purchased the blond, blue-eyed Gretchen.

Other non-flour companies gave away cut-and-sew advertising dolls. Some are so seldom seen they deserve special mention.

Gretchen, circa 1949

Betty Camp and her sidekick, Billy Van, starred in this 1923 children's book, "The Adventurous Billy and Betty," from the Van Camp Products Co. Dolls of Billy and Betty likely came out about the same time as the book. Ten trademarks from Van Camp products purchased one doll. Betty is 16 1/2" tall.

Betty Van Camp, circa 1923

Arbuckle Brothers advertised a family of four nursery rhyme dolls. A set required four wrapper fronts from Seven Day Coffee and 30 cents. One doll cost only one wrapper and 10 cents.

The Westinghouse Mazda Lamp Girl named Lotta Light dates to 1945. An introduction on the cloth says, "This is the little girl you see in the Westinghouse Mazda Lamp Ads in all the leading magazines. She reminds us to buy the bulbs that give brighter light longer, and to preserve our good eyesight by using the right size Westinghouse Mazda Lamp when we read, sew and study." Lotta Light is 16" tall.

"The Adventurous Billy and Betty," 1923

Lotta Light, 1945

Arbuckle Brothers coffee nursery rhyme dolls, 1932

~ CHAPTER FOUR ~
SEA ISLAND SUGAR DOLLS

*T*wo months before the first Rag Darling doll arrived in Edmond, Oklahoma, Western Sugar Refinery in San Francisco began to copyright an unusual line of dolls to introduce to the public during the California Pacific International Exposition in 1935 and 1936. George, Sam, Scotty, Gretchen and Henry came first. More followed in time for the exposition.

The J.D. and A.B. Spreckels Co., owner of Western Sugar Refinery, hosted the lavish event in the Palace of Food and Beverages. A tropical setting was chosen to promote the dolls and the Sea Island brand of sugar. As guests crossed a gangplank and stepped onto an island, they were handed a small booklet that explained a few of the attractions waiting for them:

"Waving palms ... thatched roofs ... a volcano that flashes fire and erupts ... dolls of all nations having a real carnival!

That's the Sea Island—sweetest spot at the California Pacific International Exposition.

There's so much to see. The talking movie—White Treasure of the Sea Islands.

And the sugar exhibit! Sugar crystals, sharp-cut as diamonds—sugar in all the stages from cane to snow-white Sea Island Sugar. And one huge crystal that 'grew' for 20 years to the size of a pineapple!

And the home-made canned fruits and preserves in luscious variety!

And if you tried our Sea Island Lemonade, you'll want to enjoy it at home. Make it this way ... "

Two popular spots on the island were the puppet show and the Refreshment Hut, where 10 cents purchased lemonade and cookies or cake. The lemonade was served unsweetened so the customer could see how quickly Sea Island Sugar dissolved. Bags of sugar with the dolls on the back were available for purchase, as were already sewn and stuffed ones.

Sea Island Sugar booklet

George introduces Hula

Twenty "Dolls of All Nations" were offered at the exposition with the promise, "and more coming!" And come they did. When the series concluded, 35 dolls had been released in seven sets of five.

The first set included George the Grocer, dressed in an apron and tie like the grocer at most hometown stores. George was the spokesperson for the group and introduced one of the dolls with a message to moms:

> *Among my new dolls is a nifty*
> *With a figure terrifically shifty,*
> *She comes on the bag*
> *With the Sea Island tag,*
> *An "extra" for mothers so thrifty.*

Those who could not attend the exposition soon found out about the dolls through their local newspaper. "Ask your grocer" and "collect the whole series of free toy cut outs" alerted thrifty moms to ask for Sea Island Sugar.

OCTOBER 24, 1934

George the Grocer

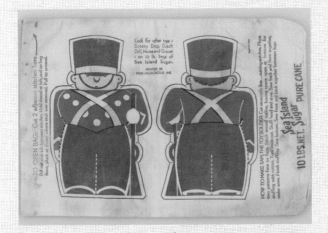

Sam the Soldier

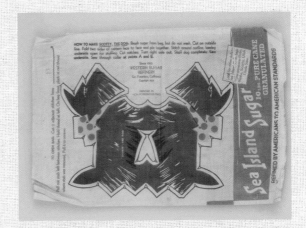

Scotty the Dog

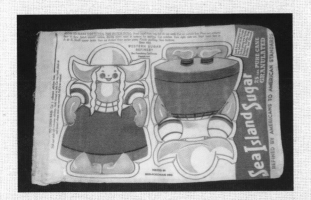

Gretchen the Dutch Doll. From the collection of
Christine Motl. Photo courtesy of Roger Nixon

Henry the Horse

MARCH 15, 1935

Fifi the French Girl

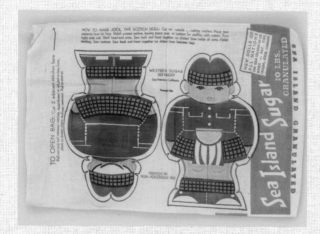

Jock the Scotch Doll

Hulda the Swedish Doll

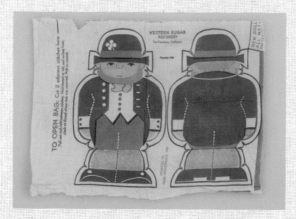

Pat the Irishman

Carmen the Spanish Girl. Collection of Edie McGinnis

JUNE 12, 1935

Tanya the Russian Girl

Chief Little Bear the Indian

Dusty the Cowboy

Hula the Sea Island Dancer

Chung the Chinese Boy

SEPTEMBER 15, 1935

Haru the Japanese Girl

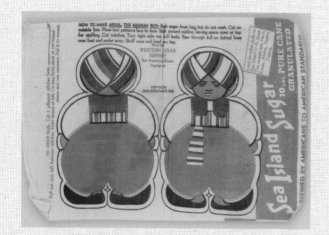

Abdul the Arabian Boy

Franz the Tyrolean Boy

Pedro the Mexican Boy

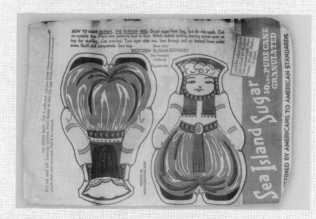

Fatima the Turkish Girl

OCTOBER 15, 1935

Uncle Sam

Gobo the South African Boy

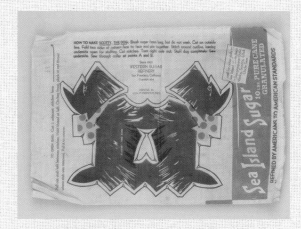

Scotty the Dog (repeat)

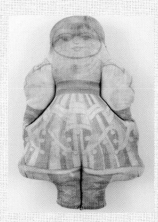

Minka the Polish Girl

Uluk the Greenland Girl

APRIL 24, 1936

Jan the Dutch Boy

Trili the Swiss Girl

Tonio the Italian Boy

Jong-Yi the Korean Girl

Ileana the Romanian Girl

OCTOBER 15, 1936

After the exposition concluded on Sept. 9, 1936, one last set was released.

Frog Who Went A-Wooing

Little Pig Who Went to Market

Little Miss Muffet

Red Riding Hood

Tommy Tucker

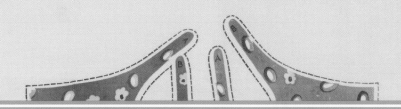

DRESS
DOLL

~ HOW TO MAKE ~

SHAKE THOROUGHLY, BUT DO NOT WASH SACK. CUT AROUND
DOTTED LINE THROUGH BOTH SIDES OF SACK. TURN IN ON
DOTTED OUTLINE OF DOLL AND SEW WITH NEEDLE AND
THREAD, LEAVING SPACE TO STUFF WITH COTTON, SAWDUST OR
SIMILAR SUBSTANCE. AFTER STUFFING, COMPLETE SEWING.

*P*romotions for a free rag doll on a sack of flour drew to a close during the 1950s. Gone were the days when millers could absorb the cost of packaging flour, feed or sugar in patterned or novelty cotton sacks. Most bag companies were already in the midst of transitioning to the more economical multiwall paper bag. From a business point of view, it was a practical and necessary change. For the customer, the time of buying a bag of flour for the doll on the back was slipping away.

Some of the large flour millers began to offer factory-sewn rag dolls. The Ceresota Flour doll, which first appeared in 1909, had at least two more runs as a cloth advertising premium and was accompanied by the Heckers doll for one of them. The dolls were shipped stuffed and ready for play.

Werthan Bag Co. of Nashville, Tennessee, was an exception and printed dolls on a few of its sacks through at least the early 1950s.

Later versions of Ceresota and Heckers Flour dolls, circa 1950-1970. Both brands of flour are still available today and sold by the Uhlmann Co.

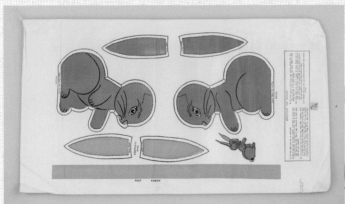

Blue Bunny Twin, King Midas Flour, King Midas Flour Mills, Minneapolis, Minnesota. Made by Werthan Bag.

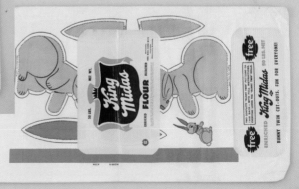

Pink Bunny Twin

Dutch Doll

Dutch Doll sack front: Carolina Beauty Flour, Carolina Feed Mills, Cheraw, South Carolina. Made by Werthan Bag.

Unnamed Pilgrim Doll, 1952

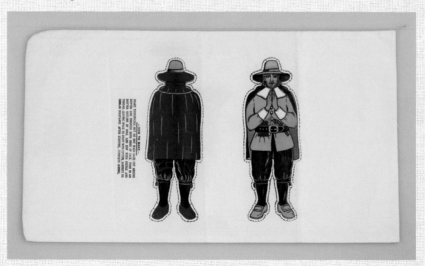

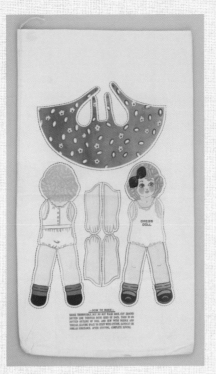

Pilgrim Doll sack front: Suretest Flour, Southern Flour Mills Inc., Albemarle, North Carolina. Made by Werthan Bag.

Unnamed Dress Doll

Front: Premium Flour, Southern Flour Mills Inc., Albemarle, North Carolina. The sack was made by Werthan Bag.

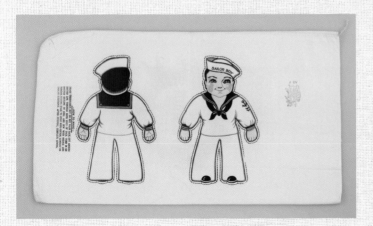

Sailor Boy, Premium Flour, Southern Flour Mills Inc.

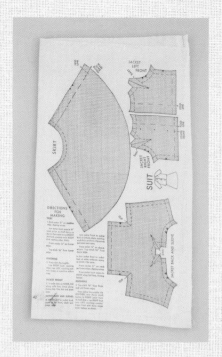

Wendy Werthan suit

Wendy Werthan evening sheath dress

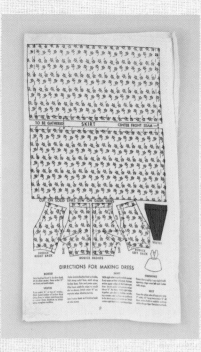

Wendy Werthan dress

Betty Ballard fashion doll

It was likely between 1960 and 1965 when Werthan printed cut-and-sew doll dresses on 10-pound sacks of flour. A coupon attached to the sack gave instructions for ordering a Wendy Werthan teenage fashion doll to wear the clothes. Wendy was 11" tall and nearly identical to the recently released Barbie doll.

Flour miller Ballard & Ballard of Louisville, Kentucky, offered what is probably the same doll as Wendy under the name Betty Ballard. Betty—"the real-live beautiful doll with arms, legs and head that move"—came in a box with a wardrobe of swimsuit, high-heel slippers, jewelry and nylons. A reminder on the box side read, "Smart dress patterns printed on back of 10 lb. Ballard Flour sacks. Yours FREE with purchase of flour." Just like Wendy and Barbie, the Betty doll could be purchased in several hair colors and bathing suit styles.

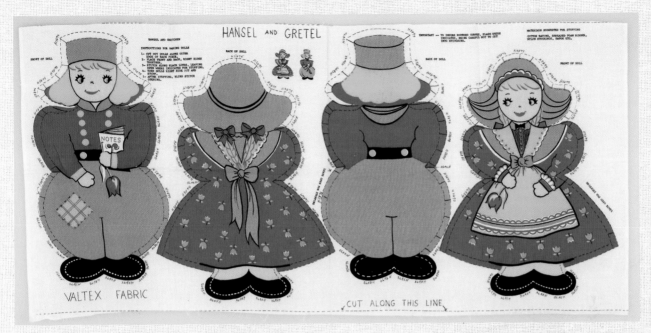

Hansel and Gretel, 36" selvage
width, Valtex Fabric

Interest in the cut-and-sew doll showed no sign of waning. As bag companies phased them out entirely or switched production to ready-made versions, fabric manufacturers began printing bright, colorfast, modern dolls on fabric available on bolts at the local department store. Cinderella, Goldilocks and the Three Bears, Pinocchio and many other favorites returned on cloth. A new era for the rag doll began.

Little Miss Sunbeam from the bakers of Sunbeam Bread, made by Chase Bag Co., circa 1960-1970. Chase Bag quickly became a leader in ready-made, cloth advertising dolls.

Jack and Jill, 35" selvage width, manufacturer unknown

Cut-and-sew doll clothes by the yard, 35/36" wide

A second colorway. The dresses have a finished length of 7-8".

TOM
The Piper's Son

Each Doll
14½ in. High

MARY and Her Lamb

JACK

Each Doll
14½ in. High

JILL

C-I-E

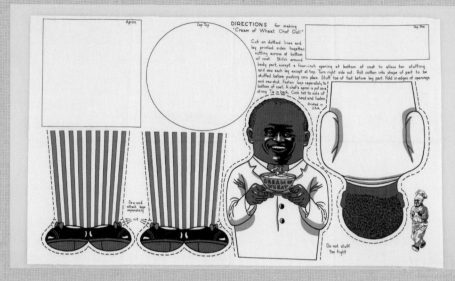

DIRECTIONS for making
"Cream of Wheat Chef Doll"

Cut on dotted lines and lay printed sides together, cutting across at bottom of coat. Stitch around body part, except a four-inch opening at bottom of coat to allow for stuffing and sew each leg except at top. Turn right side out. Roll cotton into shape of part to be stuffed before pushing into place. Stuff toe of foot before leg part. Fold in edges of openings and sew shut. Fasten legs separately to bottom of coat. A chef's apron is put on a string. Tie in back. Cook hat to side of head and fasten.

Printed in U.S.A.

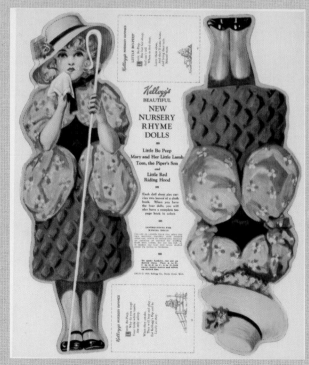

Kellogg's
BEAUTIFUL
NEW NURSERY RHYME DOLLS

- Little Bo Peep
  Mary and Her Little Lamb
  Tom, the Piper's Son
- Little Red Riding Hood

Cut out on black line.
Place back and front together with colored sides out.
Sew on dotted line, leaving top open for stuffing. (Use buttonhole stitch.)
Stuff all parts of doll to desired thickness.
Sew up opening and trim.

Designed by
Lisbeth Lofgren.

Distributed by the makers of
COCO-WHEATS
and
Miracle MAIZE

Kellogg's NURSERY RHYMES

Kellogg's
BEAUTIFUL
NEW
NURSERY
RHYME
DOLLS

Little Bo Peep
Mary and Her Little Lamb
Tom, the Piper's Son
and
Little Red
Riding Hood

MARY HAD A LITTLE LAMB

BIBLIOGRAPHY

CHAPTER 1

Ada S. Ballin, "What To Buy and Where To Buy," *Womanhood: The Magazine of Woman's Progress and Interests - Political, Legal, Social, and Intellectual - And of Health and Beauty Culture*. Volume XII, No. 62, January 1904, pages 120-121. books.google.com/books

The Delineator: An Illustrated Magazine of Literature and Fashion. Volume 60, Issue 6, Butterick Publishing Co., 1902, page 1077. books.google.com/books

Dominion (New Zealand), *Dean's True-To-Life Rag Dolls advertisement*. Volume 13, Issue 65, Dec. 10, 1919, page 6.

Samuel Adams Drake, *Nooks and Corners of the New England Coast*. Harper & Brothers, 1875, page 290.

Alice More Earle, *Child Life in Colonial Days*. Macmillan Co., November 1899, page 366 and photo facing page 370.

Eliza Leslie, *The American Girl's Book: Or, Occupation for Play Hours*. Munroe and Francis, 1831, pages 287-293. books.google.com/books

memorialhall.mass.edu/collection/itempage.jsp?itemid=5023

pilgrimhallmuseum.org/mary_chilton.htm

Josiah Howard Temple and George Sheldon, *A History of the Town of Northfield, Massachusetts: For 150 Years, With an Account of the Prior Occupation of the Territory by the Squakheags, and With Family Genealogies*. J. Munsell, 1875.

CHAPTER 2

Advertisement, "Aunt Jemima dolls free!" *The Minneapolis (Minn.) Journal*. Oct. 12, 1906.

Advertisement, "Aunt Jemima has arrived in town," *San Antonio (Texas) Daily Light*. Jan. 20, 1892.

Advertisement, "Aunt Jemima pancake flour for delicious cakes," *Omaha (Neb.) Daily Bee*. Dec. 21, 1890.

Advertisement, "Aunt Jemima's Rag Doll," *Iowa State Bystander*, Des Moines, Iowa. Nov. 17, 1905.

Advertisement, "Do you like hot pancakes in the morning?" *San Antonio (Texas) Daily Light*. Jan. 30, 1892.

Advertisement, "Send us 4 c in stamps for life history of Aunt Jemima," *Omaha (Neb.) Daily Bee*. Dec. 7, 1895.

Advertisement, "To use it once is to use no other," *Burlington (Iowa) Hawk Eye*. Nov. 11, 1891.

Advertisement, "We want every little boy and girl to have an Aunt Jemima doll," *Evening Star*, Washington, D.C. Dec. 14, 1906.

Agriculture of Pennsylvania: Containing Reports of the State Board of Agriculture, the State Agricultural Society, the State Dairymen's Association, the State Fruit Growers' Association and the State College, For 1878. 1879. books.google.com/books

"Among the Mills," *The Roller Mill*. Volume 16, April 1898.

J. H. Beadle, "Chicago Is Level: Monotonous to People from Hilly Countries," *Bismarck (N.D.) Weekly Tribune*. August 1893.

The Commissioners of Patents' Journal, Great Britain. Patent Office. 1878.

"A Delightful Resort: One of the Big Attractions at the Exposition," *Pittsburg (Pa.) Dispatch*. Sept. 15, 1889.

Waldon Fawcett, "Newspaper Ads Won Court Victory for 'Aunt Jemima' Trade Mark," *Editor & Publisher*. Vol. 53, No. 45, April 9, 1921.

"Heavy Failure at St. Joseph: R.T. Davis Company Attributes Its Insolvency to Kansas City Flood Losses," *The Kansas City Star*. Sept. 1, 1903.

M.M. Manring, *Slave in a Box: The Strange Career of Aunt Jemima*. University Press of Virginia, 1998.

Arthur F. Marquette, Brands, *Trademarks and Good Will: The Story of the Quaker Oats Company*. McGraw-Hill Inc., 1967.

Modern Packaging. Morgan-Grampian Publishing Co., Volume 23, 1950, page 319.

Official Manual of the State of Missouri for the Years 1889-90, 1889.

"The R.W. Faucett Mill Co. of St. Joseph ... Devoted to the Manufacture of Aunt Sallie Pancake Flour," *Index to the American Miller*. Mitchell Bros. Co., Volume 23, 1895, page 920.

sos.mo.gov

"S.S. Marvin and Co.'s Pan Cake Flour," *Fort Wayne (Ind.) Daily Sentinel*. Nov. 26, 1878.

Jean Williams Turner, *Collectible Aunt Jemima: Handbook & Value Guide*. Schiffer Publishing Ltd., 1994.

CHAPTER 3

Advertisement, "Help yourself to health," W.K. Kellogg's, *The Farmer's Wife*. May 1926.

Advertisement, "Puppet doll stage," *Mitchell (S.D.) Daily Republic*. Nov. 11, 1937.

Omaha (Neb.) Daily Bee. Oct. 5, 1908.

The Edmond Sun, Edmond, Okla., Territory. Vol. 17, No. 42, Ed. 1, April 25, 1906.

Stan Hoig, *Edmond: The First Century*. Edmond Historic Preservation Trust,

University of Oklahoma Press, 1987, page 19.

Frederick L. Johnson, "Professor Anderson's 'Food Shot From Guns,'" *Minnesota History* 59. No. 1 (Spring 2004), pages 4-16.

kellogghistory.com/history.html

mnopedia.org/person/anderson-alexander-p-1862-1943.

CHAPTER 4

Balboa Park History, Notes, 1935, sandiegohistory.org/amero/notes-1935new.htm

sandiegohistory.org/calpac/35expoh3.htm

Untitled advertising booklet, Western Sugar Refinery. San Francisco, California, 1935.